CATULLUS

CATULLUS

edited
with introduction, translation,
and notes by

G. P. GOOLD

DUCKWORTH

First published in 1983 by
Gerald Duckworth & Co. Ltd.
The Old Piano Factory
43 Gloucester Crescent, London NW1

© 1983 by G. P. Goold

ISBN 0 7156 1435 5 (cased)

British Library Cataloguing in Publication Data

Catullus, Gaius Valerius
    Catullus
    I. Goold, G. P.
    871'.01   PA6274
    ISBN 0–7156–1435–5

Filmset in Great Britain by
Latimer Trend & Company Ltd, Plymouth
and printed by Redwood Burn Limited, Trowbridge

Contents

Preface

THIS book is designed for all who wish to enjoy Catullus: students, scholars, lovers of literature, the inquisitive. I hope that even those with small Latin will by means of this edition come to know and prize the poet.

Most editions of Catullus are ugly, with poems and even stanzas and couplets sliced between pages, the text disfigured by obeli, angle-brackets, lacunas, and worse. In this everything has been subordinated to the artistic presentation of his work: within the limits of a page every poem is presented to the eye intact, and the only typographical device which may disturb is the footnote font to signal illustrative supplements of verses which are lost.

It is my boast that the text here presented is truer to Catullus' words than any ever yet printed. He is one of the most controversial of Latin authors: much given here will be found to vary from the standard editions as also from my own previously expressed views whenever I have discovered or been persuaded that they were wrong. The translation is neither poetry nor verse, but it aims at combining accuracy, clarity, and elegance in rendering the meaning of the Latin, while the introduction and annotations comprise the maximum amount of relevant knowledge that yet will not overwhelm the poet whose book this really is. Scholars are likely to find the pages on metre didactic and superficial: I hopefully ask their indulgence for this attempt at practical aid for those who need it.

My debts to past and present scholars and translators so outweigh any original contributions of mine as to be total; they are so many that to list them would have been ostentatious. The most important are implicit in the short bibliography or are indicated elsewhere. But I should especially like to thank Professor Otto Skutsch for helpful consultations generously given over many years and Colin Haycraft for his unfailing encouragement and patronage of this enterprise.

G.P.G.

Introduction

Row us out from Desenzano, to your
    Sirmione row!
So they row'd, and there we landed—
    'O venusta Sirmio!'
There to me thro' all the groves of
    olive in the summer glow,
There beneath the Roman ruin where
    the purple flowers grow,
Came that 'Ave atque Vale' of the
    Poet's hopeless woe,
Tenderest of Roman poets nineteen-
    hundred years ago,
'Frater Ave atque Vale'—as we
    wander'd to and fro
Gazing at the Lydian laughter of
    the Garda Lake below
Sweet Catullus's all-but-island,
    olive-silvery Sirmio!

Tennyson

NO Roman poet weaves a more binding spell upon the imagination than Catullus. Intense with the simple emotions of joy and sorrow, anger and above all love, his poems have contrived to enshrine for ever the immediacy of the moment which gave them birth. His was a transcendent fate: the mirror of his experience, however illusory, which his art so vividly conjures up before our eyes, can never be shattered by the hammer of reality (if indeed *sub specie aeternitatis* his poetry is less real than his existence), for of his historical life we know little or nothing.

Jerome records that Catullus was born in Verona and died in Rome at the age of thirty; confirmation comes partly from the poet and partly from Ovid's reference to him as dying young

(*Amores* 3.9.61f). Unfortunately, Jerome specifies the dates as 87–57 B.C., forcing us to demur, because several poems cannot possibly have been written before 55/54 and one (LIII) is fairly securely tied to August 54. However, the matter is resolved by the observation that Cinna was consul both in 87 and in 84: let the poet be born not *consule Cinna* but *consule Cinna iv*, i.e. 84 B.C., and he will die thirty years old in 54 B.C. The amendment can be regarded as certain. From 54 onwards stirring events were galvanizing the Roman world, and Catullus' was a clear and unfaltering voice: had he lived, it would have been raised, and posterity would have heard.

Beyond this simple foundation, which sheds no light on the poet's character or personality, our historical sources have little to tell us. We learn from Suetonius that when during his Gallic campaigns Julius Caesar sojourned in Verona he was accustomed to enjoy the hospitality of Catullus' father. This by itself bespeaks standing and wealth, and the impression of ample means is increased by Catullus' casual mention of a house in Rome (LXVIII A 34) and villas at Sirmio (XXXI) and Tibur (XLIV). What a pity it is that Nepos' correspondence with Cicero has perished—it is unthinkable that our hero did not figure in it. In one respect this has proved a blessing: it enables us, in fact it forces us, to surrender ourselves to the make-belief of Catullus' poems and to accept what we find therein as the historical record we have lost.

Catullus (like Ovid) was in his youth bereft of an elder brother; and it seems a strange coincidence that the latter died in Bithynia, the very province in which the poet served for a year (57–56) on the governor's staff. Wiseman makes the attractive suggestion that the Catulli may have derived their wealth from tax-farming in and exporting from that province: that would explain not only the brother's presence there, but also the poet's choice of overseas service and, more than that, his constant use of the commercial language of profit and loss and application of terms like 'pledge' and 'contract' to personal relationships (*JRS* 69 [1979] 168). It was conceivably on another occasion that

Catullus visited his brother's grave in Bithynia, but, to judge from his obvious relief to get away from it in 56 and from his omission to refer to a second journey, exceedingly improbable. This does not prove that poems LXV and LXVIII, in which he represents himself as prostrated with grief at his bereavement, were written before 57, but it certainly renders any other assumption less likely.

The most celebrated theme in the poems is Catullus' love for a woman he calls Lesbia; she was beautiful, charming, intelligent, high-born. She was also married. They became lovers, and when her husband died, the poet prayed that she would marry him. He was soon disabused of his hopes. In any case, he had been superseded. A quarrel ensued, and heartbreak.

Catullus' Lesbia, like Shakespeare's Hamlet, is an artist's creation; the name (woman of Lesbos), alluding to Sappho and identifying Catullus' sweetheart with her in his first approach (LI), is poetic only and not a real name like Caesar, Calvus, Cicero, and others whom Catullus mentions. Nevertheless, in LXXIX he disclosed to his contemporaries that Lesbia was a pseudonym for one of the three Clodia sisters; which one, they can hardly have failed to guess. That she had been the wife of Quintus Metellus Celer emerges unmistakably from her affair with Caelius Rufus (LXXVII; *Pro Caelio*) and from her connection with Gellius (see Annotation on LXXIV). Thus they will have surmised that the poet first set eyes on her in Verona in 62, when Metellus was proconsular governor of Cisalpine Gaul, or, if not then, in Rome a year or two later (Metellus was consul in 60 and died in 59). In LXVIII B Catullus revealed how he was enabled to meet her, and also that his happiness was abruptly terminated by the news of his brother's death in Bithynia, a tragedy for the family which forced him to return for a while to Verona. On resuming residence in Rome he found that his worst fears had been realized. Poem XXXVI suggests that after Catullus' year abroad Lesbia made overtures to him for a renewal of their association. He was powerless to resist. But the sequel was a repetition of what had occurred before; moreover, she was not

only unfaithful to him, but distributed her favours in a shame-
fully promiscuous way. Discarded a second time, he finally
committed himself, though only after much agonizing, to an
irrevocable renunciation.

Such, then, is the love-story of Catullus and his sweetheart. It
does not depend for its truth or validity upon historical fact. To
insist upon the total historicity of Catullus' poems about her
would be absurd. We may regard as fact, since Catullus has told
us so, that Lesbia was created out of Clodia Metelli; but beyond
that lie quicksands for the critic. Not a shred of evidence exists to
confirm the liaison between Clodia and the poet. Even so, the
involvement of Caelius (who was historically involved) and the
parade of deception over the assistance given by Allius (the
historical Manlius)—to leave entirely out of account the con-
viction Catullus implants in us that his was a real experience—
are likely to persuade us that Lesbia was in her earthly existence a
woman of flesh and blood whom we can actually name, as we can
name the mortal heroine of Verdi's *La Traviata*. Yet it is doubtful
that we have gained anything from the knowledge.

Whereas in the Lesbia poems we are at liberty to identify
Catullus the man and Catullus the poet, we are debarred from
doing so in the context of his obscene compositions. Here he is
quite emphatic (XVI 5f) in dissociating his conduct in private life
from his conduct as a poetic *persona*; and in the light of this it
would be ridiculous to make any inference about Catullus' daily
round from any lewdness encountered in his *oeuvre*. He explains
this element as justified by the wit (*lepos*) and spice (*sal*) it
provides. No doubt he deliberately sought to shock his readers by
his outspokenness and the free rein he gave to his imagination, as
when, for example, he abuses politicians. Yet it needs to be said
that Catullus' references to sex are clear and explicit; his work is
devoid of the sniggering innuendo characteristic of the music-hall
blue joke, a consideration which alone suffices to scout the
preposterous notion that the *passer* of II and III is not really
Lesbia's sparrow but symbolically represents the poet's organ.

In comparison with the brief compass of the poems the

diversity of the social life and the circle of acquaintances depicted therein are remarkable. Apart from a coterie of close but undistinguished friends (Veranius, Fabullus, Flavius) and some questionable characters like Aurelius and sundry females importuned or vilified, Catullus enjoyed close association with the nobles Manlius (LXVIII) and Caelius (LVIII); and adequate confirmation that he moved in high society flows from the references to personal contact—however slight—with Cicero and Caesar and Memmius. But what is most impressive is the list of literary men whom he addresses as intimates: Nepos and Hortensius, and more particularly the poets Valerius Cato, Cinna, Cornificius, Furius Bibaculus, Quintilius Varus, and (perhaps his closest friend) Licinius Calvus. This group, often known as the neoterics ('mod poets') after a sneering remark by Cicero, constitutes an important landmark in the history of Latin literature, rather like the *Pléiade* in sixteenth-century France: they are important not so much for their work (only that of Catullus survives) as for the literary revolution they effected, which paved the way for Virgil, Horace, and the Augustan elegists.

Earlier poets from Ennius onwards had successfully clothed Greek literary forms in a Latin dress but had conspicuously failed to match their originals in elegance and beauty of language. This failure the neoterics sought to redeem, taking as their models the poetry of Ptolemaic Alexandria and of Callimachus in particular. They imitated not only formal features like artistic word-order and prosodical precision but also the poetic ideology of their models, who discarded the major genres of drama and epic in favour of compositions on a smaller and even miniature scale, for in these every line and every word could be carefully crafted and the proportions of the whole meticulously calculated. No less did the neoterics cultivate the recondite learning characteristic of the Hellenistic poets and especially the subjective and personal manner in which they recounted abstruse and often novel versions of mythological stories.

Catullus' technical skill is especially noticeable in his handling

of the native Roman artifice of matching sound to sense: this
abounds in his work and is the more effective for being mostly
unobtrusive, like the monosyllables of III 11 with their voiceless
consonants mimicking the pathetic hopping of the sparrow along
the road of death or the alliteration, variety of vowels, and
spondaic ending of LXV 23 which arrestingly reproduce the
tumbling down of the apple that reveals all. How endearingly in
XLV does Septimius alliterate to Acme with *p* and she to him with
s, though the latter letter spits out savageness at XLIV 155f and the
former pours forth poison from the first to the last line of XXIX!
Some of his rhetorical figures are possibly overdone, anaphora,
for instance, of which he was inordinately fond, though in LXIII
(21ff *ubi*, 63f and 68ff *ego*) we should make allowances for the
constraints of the metre.

Two features of Catullus' diction call for comment. Dim-
inutives constituted a rich source of expression in colloquial Latin
no less than in modern Italian—how rich we can surmise from
the vast yield from our exiguous means of access to it: Plautus and
Terence, Cicero's *Letters*, and Petronius. On one occasion (XXV)
Catullus used these forms to great effect, exploiting the notion of
effeminacy which lurks in their nature; and elsewhere we find in
isolation over seventy different diminutives, a greater proportion
than any other classical Latin poet has put in his work. Munro
deeply regretted the Augustans' banishment of this word-type,
which 'made the lyric of the heart impossible'. Yet a little
investigation shows that in Catullus the diminutive is often
hardly more than a substitute for the natural word, which we
discover to be excluded by the metre (e.g. LXI 174 *bracchiolum* for
-chium; LXIII 35 *lassulae* for *lassae*; LXVI 16 *lacrimulis* for *-mis*; LXVIII 2
epistolium for *-tulam*): V and VII and VIII and XI and XIV and XXXI
and XXXIV and LI—to give a representative selection—scarcely
support Munro's contention.

Compound words, which contributed so much to the richness
of Greek, were coldly regarded in classical Latin. Early re-
publican poets had freely imitated Greek formations, but how
incompatible these were with the very nature of Latin is sharply

revealed by an instance like Pacuvius' *Nerei repandirostrum incurvicervicum pecus* (of dolphins). If this sounds grotesque to us, we should reflect that compounds like Ennius' *altivolans* and Lucretius' *lauricomus* (which may appeal to us as highly poetical) probably struck the Romans as being unattractive only in a lesser degree. In fact the only compounds to become thoroughly at home in Latin were noun-object/verb combinations like *signifer*. In his lyrics Catullus has only *buxifer, laserpicifer, pinnipes*, and *plumipes* (the last two in the experimental LV), and they are seen no more; of the other dozen examples *erifuga, hederiger, nemorivagus, properipes*, and *silvicultrix* all occur in LXIII and, since they can never enter dactylic verse, probably owe their existence in some measure to metrical exigencies.

The most impressive feature of Catullus' diction, however, is— and here one can do no better than quote from the old school edition (1879) of Francis P. Simpson—'the simplicity and naturalness of his language, which are in great contrast to the later artificial Latin style ... However difficult the metre in which he writes, however subtle the thought he would convey, he is never intricate and never obscure. His words seem to have fallen of themselves into metre without leaving their natural order, and would make good prose—if they were not poetry. His language, in the epigrams, lyrics, and elegiacs, is little removed from ordinary speech. He is full of familiar phrases ... He uses the tongue of the wits of the town, the lips of the lover of real life.'

His humanity needs no comment, but he stands out above most poets of antiquity for his imaginative sympathy with nature and inanimate things. Though his zest for society took him to Rome he never lost his appreciation of the north Italian scenery which we may fancy we detect in such passages as the third stanza of XXXIV and the first major simile of LXVIII (57ff). In particular the sea, indeed water generally, which for Lucretius, Virgil, Horace, and the other poets was an element to be feared and shunned, represents for Catullus laughter and gaiety (XXXI 14; LXIV 269ff). For him the lopping of a wild-flower was as tragic as the destruction of his own love (XI 22ff), a sensitivity he displays again in LXII (39ff).

The verse of Catullus so often implies a situation in which individual poems were sent on tablets (XLII) or in *feuilleton* (XXXV) that it must have been in this way that the poet's productions were first disseminated and that he himself acquired some celebrity or, it may be, notoriety (XVI 12, referring to V 10). We also read of reactions experienced on receipt or in the circulation of his poems whether by intimates like Lesbia (XXXVI) or Cornelius Nepos (I) or by prominent public figures like Cicero (XLIX) or Caesar (LIV). 'Children of the moment' was the happy phrase that Wilamowitz applied to such poems, and it accurately conveys how little at the time of creation the poet was concerned with publication in book-form. That could come later. The tantalizing thing is we do not know how far Catullus was able, to use the modern term, to see his work through the press. He cannot have done more than assemble a collection of his lyrics and prefix a dedication to Cornelius Nepos when death overtook him (and of this he may have had no warning). Improbable even that this lyric collection was published as such: antiquity has no knowledge of a title, and it may be wondered whether, if 'publication' (that is the establishment of a definitive edition) had already taken place, the person responsible for the collected edition which we inherit today would have ventured to insert other poems into it, as he seems to have done. The last year of Catullus' life was prolific, but he died with his work unfinished: his epyllion lacks a title and may lack the author's *imprimatur* as well; nor do the long elegiacs either form a whole or amount to sufficient bulk to constitute a *libellus* on their own. In short, Catullus' poems were published posthumously. Further evidence and argument tending to this conclusion are mentioned at relevant places in the annotations.

At the end of his novel Sir Pierson Dixon casts Gaius Helvius Cinna as the posthumous editor, depicting him as being in close touch with Catullus at the time of his death and privy to the poet's plan to embark on the publication of a selection of his verse. This is possible enough, though, if we are to hazard a guess, we may with Pighi believe Cornelius Nepos (CII) to be a more likely candidate. Still, that the editor undertook the task at once seems on a number of counts fairly certain, not least because a definitive text was indeed published, and the later one puts this event, the more difficult it is to imagine it happening at all. Furthermore, only an immediate edition will adequately account for the considerable influence which Catullus exercised on the Augustan poets, not merely on the naturally sympathetic elegists, but on Virgil and Horace, too, whose proud characters found it easy to borrow from the poet of Verona but impossible to make a bow of acknowledgement to him. Catullus' was not a suitable text for prescription in the school syllabus: there was hence no academic demand for copies, and none for a commentary; as a result his book became a rarity. The walls of Pompeii, that eloquent testimony to the power of the classics curriculum to preserve and propagate, amply attest the survival of Rome's other great poets, but not Catullus. Not a single quotation, and amid so much scatological verse not a single hendecasyllable! The fate of Catullus henceforth is a fight against odds, which time after time he seems to have lost, only to find some unexpected means of recovery. Often enough we encounter some mention of his name, a quotation even, but seldom with any assurance that our source has the custody of his text: Gellius, Servius, Priscian, Isidore have lost contact with the poet and know of him only what they have come across in others. We must rather look for evidence of his lifeline in non-academic writers, but after Martial the trail soon peters out: apart from Ausonius and Paulinus, who between them confirm that a copy had reached Bordeaux, there is nothing to suggest that the *Liber Catulli* (as distinct from quotations or excerpts) was known to late antiquity. Thereafter a faint and possibly illusory echo in a poem of Heiric of Auxerre (*c.* 873) and an unequivocal one in William of Malmesbury (*c.* 1120) remain as the total impact of Catullus on the literature of the Middle Ages.

The will-o'-the-wisp quality which attaches to the survival of the poet's memory is naturally reflected in an elusive manuscript tradition. Sometime perhaps as early as the sixth century (thither points a parallel in Venantius Fortunatus) the hexameter epithalamium (LXII) was excerpted from a complete manuscript of Catullus to form part of an anthology (Weinreich believes that the poem was selected as suitable for setting to music in a choral arrangement); and as a result our first extant witness to the text is the codex Thuaneus of the late ninth century (*T*: probably written at Tours, now in the Bibliothèque Nationale). Several remarkable errors which *T* has in common with the mainstream tradition (notably the lacuna after verse 32) prove beyond doubt that its text derives from some pre-archetypal ancestor of our complete manuscripts.

Hardly a century later, in 966, Bishop Rather of Verona refers to a Catullus in his possession, which (whether he found it in the Capitular Library or brought it with him) probably originated in Burgundy. But with this tantalizingly brief notice the curtain of oblivion once more descends upon our poet's name and remains lowered for several centuries. Then, in the opening years of the fourteenth century—an aura of mystery obscures what happened—Verona is a second time blessed with the epiphany of a manuscript of Catullus. Was it Rather's? No: from palaeographical errors in the tradition Professor Julian Brown deduces that this manuscript (*V*) was written (probably in France) in protogothic script of the late twelfth century. In any case, we are obliged to recognize that *V* had only recently been brought back to Verona from exile in a distant land, as some verses written on the manuscript (and preserved in its descendants) assert. Of course, *V* may have been a copy of Rather's codex; and if it was not, it must have been a close relative, for it is unlikely in the extreme that there existed *two* medieval traditions of Catullus. Not much later than 1310 *V* was used and quoted by Benzo of Alessandria, and then by Hieremias de Montagnone; a Veronese anthology produced in 1329 quotes from poem XXII, and in the next decade or two *V* is being read by Guglielmo da Pastrengo of Verona and, more notably, was in a copy (*X*) transcribed for and possibly by Guglielmo's friend Petrarch, very likely when he visited Verona in 1345.

About 1370, it seems, a second copy of *V* was made, *O* (codex Oxoniensis); and on Petrarch's death in 1374 his Catullus (*X*) emerged from long disuse and the following year was transcribed in two copies: *G* (codex Sangermanensis: now in the Bibliothèque Nationale) and—a little later, perhaps in the same year—*R* (codex Romanus, made for Coluccio Salutati: now in the Vatican). Thus the survival of Catullus, which from the very inditement of the *Cui dono lepidum* had been so precarious and even ill-starred a prospect, was ensured for ever. But it was a close call. Shortly after surrendering their charge *V* and *X* disappear and are heard of no more.

Between the manuscripts *OGR* and the first printed edition (1472) about a hundred copies were made (*R* is the principal transmitter, and it may here be remarked that different sorts of variant readings and conjectures entered in *R* have created intricate stemmatological problems for investigators), but as witnesses of an authentic tradition these are dispensable: our total inheritance of the text of Catullus from antiquity is contained in *OGR*; all other manuscripts, all printed editions even, are dependent on these three. Of course, the renaissance manuscripts are not to be dismissed as worthless: in fact they constitute a valuable repository of emendations, for the transmitted text had over the span of 1350 years contracted about a thousand errors, superficial for the most part though requiring effort, sometimes a good deal of acumen as well, to detect and repair. While this repair work naturally cannot be properly assessed on a numerical basis and while no critic can arrogate to himself more than a fallible authority in pronouncing on error and the correction thereof, yet a general calculation presents a most instructive picture.

In the century which elapsed from the transcription of *OGR* to the impact of printing on the tradition Italian scholars, for the most part unidentifiable, corrected the text in some 460 places; then thirty years of incunabula from the *editio princeps* to the

Aldine increased the total count to very nearly 700. This purification of the text, nowadays taken for granted, stands as a splendid tribute to the enthusiasm and genius of renaissance humanism. Thereafter, as the more glaring errors are removed, leaving the less obvious and intractable undetected or unsolved, the tally of successes naturally diminishes: the sixteenth century (from 1503) claims 85, the seventeenth only 37, and the eighteenth a mere 16. In the nineteenth, however, the pre-dominance of classics in the curriculum and, especially, the glorious age of German scholarship are strikingly reflected in 147 corrections contributed by thirty-five individuals. Until 1829 editors had been content to adopt any readng which appealed to their taste regardless of what manuscript happened to furnish it. In that year Karl Lachmann (the foremost Latinist of the century) first applied science and method to the editing of Catullus: taking five manuscripts as the most authoritative guide to the tradition he founded his text on those and gave complete reports of two. But though Lachmann's choices were not bad, they were not the best; and it fell to Emil Baehrens to effect in 1876 the decisive break-through with an edition based on G (first used by Sillig in 1830) and O (brought to light by Robinson Ellis in 1867). If his text is marred by many unnecessary or improbable conjectures, nevertheless his apparatus criticus is a model of editorial technique and virtually put the archetype into the reader's hands. This work must be carefully distinguished from K. P. Schulze's revision of it in 1893, an atrocious performance which altered or eliminated everything that was excellent in it and thoroughly merited the severe castigation meted out by A. E. Housman (*CR* 8 [1894] 251ff).

The last of the principal manuscripts, R, was identified as such (having previously been miscatalogued in the Vatican Library) in 1896 by Professor W. G. Hale. Over sixty years went by before its readings were incorporated in an edition, but in truth little of it remained to be revealed, for the two branches of the stemma were already represented by O and G, and most of the renaissance manuscripts had derived their texts from R or its apographs. So far the twentieth century has seen some 30 plausible emendations put forward, but by now we are approaching the limit of what we can hope to accomplish. Not that nothing is left to be done, for even when true readings have been found (or false readings exposed) it often takes ages to establish (or disestablish) them—a glance at the first poem will illustrate both points; and in the matter of interpretation there is no end.

If textual problems have in the past left much of Catullus' work obscure and unfocused, this has never affected his popularity or his power to influence others. Indeed, the last five centuries have responded to him a good deal more than did ancient Rome. His effect on Petrarch is, it is true, less than one would have expected, but we are ignorant of the extent of his acquaintance with Catullus and know merely the fact of it. But with the printed book the poet spreads like wild-fire. Ariosto, for example, borrows the simile of the flower and the virgin in LXII 39ff for the first canto of *Orlando Furioso*; a little later Tasso takes it for the *Gerusalemme Liberata* (XVI 14), whence Edmund Spenser has made a close version for his *Faerie Queene* (II 74f), not however deterring Ben Jonson from slipping a faithful translation of the original into his play *The Barriers*. In contemporary France Ronsard and his fellow lyrists showed themselves no less susceptible to the magic of the new-found Orpheus, as the following verses of De Baïf illustrate:

> Sus larmoyez Amourettes,
> O Mignardises tendrettes,
> Sus larmoyez tendrement.
> Le passereau de m'amie:
> Le pauvret n'est plus en vie,
> Le pauvret qu'elle aimait mieux
> Que la clarté de ses yeux.

By 1803, François Noël could list no less than thirty renditions in French verse of *Vivamus, mea Lesbia*.

Catullus' influence in England begins with something of a puzzle, for, while no one doubts that John Skelton's *Book of Philip*

Sparrow (*c.* 1505: of 1382 lines!) draws somehow for its theme upon the poet of Verona, we look in vain for an incontrovertible piece of evidence which could clinch the connection. Simply in themselves translations are not perhaps the surest index of a poet's worth or influence, but Catullus has too long and distinguished a band of English admirers not to have a few of them indicated here: James Elroy Flecker (IV), Crashaw (V), Campion (VIII), John Hookham Frere (X), Leigh Hunt (XXXVIII), Cowley (XLV), Lovelace (XLVIII), Gladstone (LI), Sir Philip Sidney (LXX), Swift (XCII). More impressive are the individual tunes, as it were, taken from Catullus and set for English song; from different lines of Poem V Christopher Marlowe and Robert Herrick reproduce the Latin to perfection:

> Come live with me and be my love . . .

and

> Give me a kiss, and to that kiss a score:
> Then to that twenty add a hundred more:
> A thousand to that hundred: so kiss on,
> To make the thousand up a million.

And it is surely not fanciful to hear a bar of Catullus' (LXXII 2) in the finest of Ben Jonson's lyrics:

> But might I of Jove's nectar sip,
> I would not change for thine.

Shakespeare's small Latin is not commonly held to have included Catullus, but the following lines from *Cymbeline* (III v 70ff) contain themes from LXXXV and LXXXVI that have no obvious connection with each other and seem to derive—it is most curious—from the Bard's knowledge of a text which presented them one after the other:

> I love and hate her: for she's fair and royal,
> And that she hath all courtly parts more exquisite
> Than any lady, winning from every one

> The best she hath, and she, of all compounded,
> Outsells them all.

The second thought recurs in *Love's Labour's Lost* (ii i 9ff):

> Be now as prodigal of all dear grace,
> As Nature was in making graces dear,
> When she did starve the general world beside
> And prodigally gave them all to you.

One hesitates to deny to Shakespeare's inexhaustible invention anything which he is not indisputably proved to have got from another; but even coincidences may have something to tell us. Certainly *Sonnet* 27 brings xxxi to mind:

> Weary with toil I haste me to my bed,
> The dear repose for limbs with travel tired.

And *Sonnet* 30, though transcending xcvi, is undoubtedly reminiscent of it. Furthermore, the dark lady of the *Sonnets* forms a striking parallel to Lesbia: both were beautiful and as treacherous to their lovers as to their husbands. We read in 18:

> Shall I compare thee to a summer's day?
> Thou art more lovely and more temperate.

But in 147 the scales have fallen from the worshipper's eyes:

> For I have sworn thee fair, and thought thee bright,
> Who art as black as hell, as dark as night.

Laurence Binyon and Ezra Pound in the twentieth century—and even more J. C. Squire ('To a Roman' 1923)—have continued to render enthusiastic homage to our poet, though perhaps it was the Victorians who did so in the most musical form: with Tennyson's lyric salutation already placed at the head of this introduction (Italians might have preferred Carducci's *Sirmione*), let Landor's epigram (worth all his criticism combined) be given here:

Tell me not what too well I know
About the bard of Sirmio—
    Yes, in Thalia's son
Such stains there are—as when a Grace
Sprinkles another's laughing face
    With nectar, and runs on.

The lack of knowledge that so tantalizingly conceals the poet's
career from our gaze has induced several modern novelists to
employ their art on drawing back the veil. Pride of place must go
to Thornton Wilder's *The Ides of March* (New York 1948). In it
several of Catullus' poems find a convincing setting, and the
author brings both him and the other characters vividly to life;
but he takes enormous liberties with history, and, as a con-
sequence, the better acquainted his readers are with the period,
the less easily will they surrender to his story. Kenneth Benton's
Death on the Appian Way (London 1974) adheres closely to known
fact, and he also engages our attention for a more interesting
reason: he portrays Catullus not as Catullus appeared to himself,
but as he appeared to Marcus Caelius (the narrator) and to
Clodia (the title of course refers to the killing of her brother). Sir
Pierson Dixon's *Farewell, Catullus* (London 1953) has already
been mentioned: his plot aims at historical accuracy; but he has
created a new character, Poppaea, a slave of Catullus, and
created her so well that the real characters rather pale beside her.

A very different attempt to revivify the poet of Verona was
made by the composer Carl Orff (1895–), a revolutionary spirit
who has consistently striven to express the basic emotions in
simple sounds and primitive rhythms. His *Trionfi* in particular
attempts to interpret in this way select poetry of the distant past;
the work is a trilogy, the first part of which, *Carmina Burana*
(1937), is probably the best known. But our concern is with the
sequel, wherein Orff sets the Latin of Catullus to music.

Part Two, *Catulli Carmina*, was first produced in Leipzig in
1943. From the orchestra pit two solo voices and an *a cappella*
chorus sing to an accompaniment of four pianos and extensive

percussion, while on the stage dancers mime the story. The chorus consists of ardent young couples together with a group of old men who, trying to convince them of the essential treachery of love, persuade them to watch a performance of 'The Poems of Catullus'. After this prelude on the proscenium the drama of the stage begins. The first act (LXXXV, V, LI, LVIII, LXX) opens with Catullus and Lesbia together, but when he has fallen asleep Lesbia leaves him to dance in a nearby tavern; on waking he is joined and consoled by Caelus (*sic*: the name should of course be Caelius). In act two (CIX, LXXIII) the poet, sleeping in the street outside Lesbia's house, dreams that he is inside sharing her bed, but presently he recognizes the lover to be not himself, but Caelus: he wakes and despairs. In the final act (XXXII, XLI, VIII, LXXXVII, LXXV) he makes an evidently unsuccessful bid for Ipsitilla's favours, and has an angry encounter with Ammiana (*sic*: our Anneiana). But Lesbia is the only woman he wants. Escorted by Caelus she finally appears, hails Catullus, but is rudely repulsed by him. We return to the outer plot: although the young people have followed the cautionary tale with rapt attention, when it is over they are once more seized with mutual desire and abandon themselves to love; the old men acknowledge the futility of further persuasion.

Part Three, *Trionfo di Afrodite* (the Italian title was occasioned by the *première* at La Scala, Milan, 1953), is a 'scenic concerto' in seven parts representing ancient wedding ritual and, on a cosmic level, the ultimate triumph of love. This portion of Orff's work is distinguished by being scored for a large orchestra—in full use throughout—of strings and winds as well as copious percussion; the vocal line ranges from chanted recitative to the most florid melismata, in insistent rhythms and repetitions redolent at once of ritual and passion. The principal texts are Catullus' epi-thalamiums, perceptively inverted so that LXII (part *i*), 'anti-phonal song to the evening star', serves as a preliminary to the actual wedding, LXI (parts *iv* and *v*). Can it be that Catullus himself conceived the poems in this relationship? The curious may wish to be told that parts *ii*, *iii*, and *vi* are settings of Sappho (in Greek) representing respectively the marriage procession, the meeting of bride and groom, and their love-duet in the bridal chamber; *vii* celebrates in words from Euripides the supreme power of Aphrodite in fulfilling the purpose of the universe.

Orff's impressive achievement notwithstanding, Catullus himself probably had no thought of his poems being set to music: he never mentions the lyre or any other stringed instrument, and those poems which refer to the composition of verses (e.g. XXII, L) or to the audience's reception of them (e.g. XVI 13, XXXV 13) tell heavily against the idea. The only clues pointing in the other direction are, with one exception, confined to the long poems. In them Catullus' declaration about 'singing songs' (LXV 12) is most naturally explained as a conventional metaphor available to any poet; and the spinning-song of the Fates in LXIV was hardly designed as a musical interlude in a non-musical epic. Although LXI and LXII are wedding-songs and are represented throughout as musical pieces, and although LXIII emphasizes the tambourine, cymbals, and Phrygian pipe of Cybele's cult and would be enhanced if sung to such an accompaniment, we look in vain for any data to show that a performance of this kind was the poet's intention.

The exception referred to above is poem XXXIV, a choral hymn seemingly found among the poet's papers and added to the collection after his death: it is the only poem in Catullus devoid of a personal reference (for LXVI is scarcely parallel), and this, added to the appeal for help in the last stanza, prompts the speculation that it was commissioned for actual performance on a public occasion. But speculation it must remain—many scholars regard the hymn as purely literary—and in the absence of further evidence we are left with the strong probability that Catullus never (well, hardly ever) conceived his poems as requiring the accompaniment of music. Nor is this an unwelcome conclusion, for it means that with just a little effort we can by the use of our own voices bring Catullus to life for ourselves.

Reading Catullus Aloud

CATULLUS should be read in Latin and aloud. If we today cannot perfectly reproduce the authentic sound of Catullus' poetry, we may easily contrive a tolerable and satisfying approximation to it.

We must remember that rhythm in classical Latin verse was determined by regular sequences, not of accented and un-accented syllables, but of syllables either long or short. In English we do not measure syllables by length, and English syllables cannot be divided into long or short: they come in an infinite range of sizes. Even accented syllables are by no means all alike or identically accented all the time. Still, we should not be afraid in reading Latin to use stress as an aid to rhythmical appreciation and to stress those syllables (hereunder marked with an acute accent) which by occurring at fixed intervals give a rhythmical beat to the utterance. Of course the sense must be heeded: punctuation within the verse may require a distinct pause (e.g. after the interrogation mark in XLII 7); lack of punctuation at the end (e.g. of XIII 3) may equally require uninterrupted delivery. And it had better be stated that the stress we are giving in this way is an artificial substitute for a pulse-beat which the Roman ear identified by syllabic length. Most Latin words have a stress-accent of their own (on the antepenult, if the penult is short, as in 1 2 *arido*; otherwise on the penult, as in 1 1 *libellum*). So we must make our metrical beat a light one (1 4 *aliquíd*, where the stress-accent is actually on the first syllable) in order to keep distortion to a minimum. But very often metrical beat and stress-accent will coincide.

In pronunciation we ought to utter pure vowels, discriminating between long and short quantity, and to sound double-consonants as such. The matter of elision requires special care. Every syllable ending in an open vowel (or the letter *m*) which precedes a word commencing with a vowel (or the letter *h*, which was scarcely sounded in classical Latin) is not considered as forming part of the metrical sequence: it is elided. From modern Italian, where the same phenomenon occurs, we may infer that the elided vowel was usually articulated, but very lightly and without taking up any metrical time; and that in common words or terminations, or where the contiguous vowels were identical, it may have been suppressed altogether. Certainly the beginner will find it easier to suppress elided vowels, thus:

> XXVI 5   o vent' horribil' atque pestilentem!

But before a pause particularly, or where it is long, an elided vowel is not likely to have been sharply clipped off. So let it be uttered quickly but distinctly in a kind of liaison with the following vowel:

> III 1   luget(e), o Veneres . . .
> X 11   . . . nam Cytori(o) in jugo

A few details:

(i) the exclamation *o* is not elided (LXI 1, etc.);

(ii) thrice a vowel is shortened, not elided: x 26 *manĕ*; LV 4 *tĕ*; XCVII 1 *dĭ*;

(iii) elision occasionally occurs in lyric metres at the end of a line (XI 19, 22; XXXIV 11, 22; LXI 115, 135, 140, 184, 227) and once at the end of a hexameter (LXIV 298).

HENDECASYLLABIC METRES

By far the greater portion of Catullus' lyrics (all as far as LVIII excepting these: IV, VIII, XI, XVII, XXII, XXV, XXIX–XXXI, XXXIV, XXXVII, XXXIX, XLIV, LIf) is composed in hendecasyllables, an eleven-syllable line normally commencing with a heavy base of two long syllables. The scheme, and Tennyson's imitation of it, are subjoined.

$$\acute{-} \quad - \qquad \acute{-} \; \cup \; \cup \; \acute{-} \qquad \cup \; \acute{-} \; \cup \; \acute{-} \; - \qquad \textit{(hendecasyllable)}$$

O you chorus of indolent reviewers,
Irresponsible, indolent reviewers,
Look I come to the test, a tiny poem
All composed in a metre of Catullus.

So Catullus' most polished hendecasyllables. In others he occasionally permits a light base, with the second syllable short.

$$\acute{-} \; \cup \qquad \acute{-} \; \cup \; \cup \; \acute{-} \qquad \cup \; \acute{-} \; \cup \; \acute{-} \; -$$

Lo, the summer is dead, the sun is faded.

And in such poems we as often encounter an initial short syllable.

$$\cup \; \acute{-} \qquad \acute{-} \; \cup \; \cup \; \acute{-} \qquad \cup \; \acute{-} \; \cup \; \acute{-} \; -$$

Alas, summer is dead, the sun is faded.

At the beginning and end of LV, however, the poet has embarked on a remarkable experiment, syncopating in alternate lines the double-short syllables of the verse.

$$\acute{-} \; - \qquad \acute{-} \; - \; \acute{-} \qquad \cup \; \acute{-} \; \cup \; \acute{-} \; - \qquad \textit{(syncop. hendec.)}$$
$$\acute{-} \; - \qquad \acute{-} \; \cup \; \cup \; \acute{-} \qquad \cup \; \acute{-} \; \cup \; \acute{-} \; -$$

Do please show me, if it's not a bother,
   Where, oh where is the hiding-place you've got to?
I've long sought you round the Lesser Campus,
   Round Great Circus and round the little chapels.

SAPPHIC STANZA

For his first and last poems to Lesbia (LI, XI) Catullus chose the Sapphic stanza: this consists of three lines of an eleven-syllable sequence (usually with a word-break after the fifth) followed by a short clausula. The scheme (with an illustration taken from Swinburne) is as follows:

1–3 $\acute\cup\;\cup\;\acute\cup\;\underset{\smile}{\cup}\;\acute\cup\;\|\quad\cup\;\cup\;\acute\cup\;\cup\;\acute\cup\;-$ (*sapphic*)

4      $\acute\cup\;\cup\;\cup\;\acute\cup\;-$ (*adonean*)

> All the night sleep came not upon my eyelids,
> Shed not dew, nor shook nor unclosed a feather,
> Yet with lips shut close and with eyes of iron
>   Stood and beheld me.

CHORIAMBIC METRES

The slight adaptation of some verses from Tennyson's 'Jubilee Ode' will serve to illustrate Catullus' use of choriambic ($-\cup\cup-$) systems.

$\acute\cup\;\underset{\smile}{\cup}\qquad\acute\cup\;\cup\;\cup\;\acute\cup\qquad\cup\;\acute\cup$ (*glyconic*)

$\acute\cup\;\underset{\smile}{\cup}\qquad\acute\cup\;\cup\;\cup\;\acute\cup\qquad-$ (*pherecratean*)

> You that wanton in affluence
> Spare not now to be bountiful,
> Call your poor to regale with you,
>   All the lowly, the hungry.

Stanzas of three glyconics and a pherecratean constitute the form of XXXIV; similar stanzas, but with four glyconics, LXI; and consecutive sequences of glyconic and pherecratean (the combination is termed a priapean), XVII.

The metre of XXX is known as the greater asclepiad: it may be regarded as a glyconic with two choriambs inserted. Swinburne

has magnificently recaptured the rhythm in English in his
'Choriambics', which begins as follows:

$$\acute{\smile} - \;\; \acute{\smile} \smile \smile \acute{\smile} \;\; \acute{\smile} \smile \smile \acute{\smile} \;\; \acute{\smile} \smile \smile \acute{\smile} \;\; \smile \acute{\smile} \qquad (greater\ asclep.)$$

Love, what ailed thee to leave life that was made
    lovely, we thought, with love?
What sweet visions of sleep lured thee away,
    down from the light above?

IAMBIC METRES

The iambic metre, a simple sequence of short and long syllables, is
the most natural of rhythms, and doubtless for this reason became
the ordinary metre of Greek and Roman drama. Poems IV and
XXIX are *tours de force*, remarkable for the unbroken sequence of
pure iambs ($\smile -$). Each line consists of six iambs, with a regular
word-break after the fifth or the seventh syllable

$$\smile \acute{\smile} \;\; \smile \acute{\smile} \;\; \smile \| \; \acute{\smile} \;\; \smile \| \; \acute{\smile} \;\; \smile \acute{\smile} \;\; \smile \acute{\smile} \qquad (iamb.\ senarius)$$

The dainty vessel yonder you, my friends, discern,
Of yachts the swiftest once upon the Hellespont.

A relaxation, however, occurs in LII, where spondees ($- -$) are
permitted in the first and third feet. It will be noticed that this
length of iambic line is foreign to English, its place being usurped
by the five-footer (as in Gray's *Elegy*).

    A further use of this rhythm is seen in XXV (iambic septe-
narius), where the strict insistence on iambs is modified in the first
foot of each half of the verse, which permits a spondee.

$$\breve{\smile} \acute{\smile} \;\; \smile \acute{\smile} \;\; \smile \acute{\smile} \;\; \smile \acute{\smile} \| \breve{\smile} \acute{\smile} \;\; \smile \acute{\smile} \;\; \smile \acute{\smile} \;\; - \qquad (iamb.\ sept.)$$

As soft as eiderdown you are, or fur of bunny rabbit,
Or lobe of ear, or spider's web, you miserable pansy.

    In eight poems (VIII, XXII, XXXI, XXXVII, XXXIX, XLIV, LIX, LX) is found a variation of the iambic senarius: in this the last foot is a spondee, producing a halting effect, which gives this metre its distinctive name, scazon (or limping iambic).

$$\cup\; \underline{}\quad \cup\; \underline{}\quad \cup\; \underline{}\quad \cup\; \underline{}\quad \cup\; \underline{}\quad \underline{}\; -$$ (*scazon*)

Ignatius is the owner of superb white teeth,
With which he gives to all he meets a big broad smile.

The short syllables in the first and third feet may be replaced by longs, and the long syllables in the second and third resolved into two shorts.

With which to ĕvĕryone he gives a big broad smile.
With which he gives to ĕvĕryone a big broad smile.

Catullus uses the limping iambic to suggest intensity in the varied emotions of despair, anger and contempt, and heartfelt relief.

GALLIAMBIC METRE

The verses of the galliambic metre (poem LXIII) consist of two cola (in this edition printed on alternate lines). The rhythm of the first is reflected in many a verse of Longfellow's *Hiawatha*:

$$\cup\; \cup\; \underline{}\; \cup\quad |\quad -\; \cup\; \underline{}\; -$$ (*anacreontic*)

In the dreadful days of Shal-shah,
In the days long since departed,
In the kingdom of the West-Wind.

The second colon is an anacreontic catalectic, that is one with the last syllable syncopated, giving for example 'In the dreadful days of yore'. But Catullus almost always resolves the fifth syllable into two shorts:

$$\cup\; \cup\; \underline{}\; \cup\quad |\quad \cup\; \cup\; \cup\; \underline{}$$ (*anacr. catalectic*)

In the long confederate lines.

Joining these two sequences we arrive at the poet's basic scheme, which may be illustrated by F. R. Dale's metrical version of lines 34–36:

> ∪ ∪ ⏓ ∪ | – ∪ ⏓ –
> ∪ ∪ ⏓ ∪ | ∪ ∪ ∪ ⏓   (*galliambic*)
>
> And with hasting feet the girl priests
>   sped along wherever he led,
> Till at last the weary band came
>   to the mighty hill of the queen,
> And from strain of toil and fasting
>   settled down in utter collapse.

We are not quite out of the wood. A number of variations are encountered (all, however, easy to appreciate): (a) the initial double-shorts may be replaced by a long, and in the second colon the original long of the fifth syllable may be restored: line 73 incorporates the three possibilities:

> – ⏓ ∪ | – ∪ ⏓ –
> – ⏓ ∪ | – ∪ ⏓
>
> Now, now I rue my action,
>   now, now do I repent.

(b) one (but only one) of the first two longs of the anacreontic may be resolved into two shorts, and so too the first long of the second colon (which must then end – ∪ –). These rhythms may be illustrated as follows:

> ∪ ∪ ∪ ∪ ∪ | – ∪ ⏓ –   (23 etc.)
> As in pitiful plaintive language

> ∪ ∪ ⏓ ∪ | ∪ ∪ ∪ ⏓ –   (4 etc.)
> In a quarrel with a delinquent

> ∪ ∪ ∪ ∪ ∪ | – ∪ ⏓   (only 91)
> very vividly came to mind

Tennyson has admirably recreated the general spirit of the galliambic metre in his experimental 'Boadicea', but his verses cannot pretend to conform to Catullus' metrical system.

DACTYLIC METRES

Dactylic metre was used in epic and epigrammatic verse in Greece from time immemorial and at Rome from the earliest days of Greek influence. The two basic lines, the hexameter and the pentameter, the former the metre of LXII and LXIV, and in combination the couplet exclusively employed in poems LXV to the end, may in their simplest form be schematized as follows:

$$\acute{-}\,\cup\,\cup \quad \acute{-}\,\cup\,\cup \quad \acute{-}\,\cup\,\cup \quad \acute{-}\,\cup\,\cup \quad \acute{-}\,\cup\,\cup \quad \acute{-}\; - \qquad (\textit{hexameter})$$
$$\acute{-}\,\cup\,\cup \quad \acute{-}\,\cup\,\cup \quad \acute{-}\,\|\; \acute{-}\,\cup\,\cup \quad \acute{-}\,\cup\,\cup \quad \acute{-} \qquad (\textit{pentameter})$$

Softly the Angelus sounded, and over the roofs of the
    village
Columns of issuing smoke rose from a hundred abodes.

The dactyl ($-\cup\cup$), however, is commonly replaced by a spondee ($--$) in any of the first four feet of the hexameter (rarely in the fifth): the following lines of Kingsley's contain some of the variations, and his first and third lines illustrate the third-foot word-break usual in Latin:

$$\acute{-}\,\cup\cup \quad \acute{-}\,\cup\cup \quad \acute{-}\,\|\,\cup\cup \quad \acute{-}\,\cup\cup \quad \acute{-}\,\cup\,\cup \quad \acute{-}\; -$$

Blissful, they turned them to go: but the fair-tressed
    Pallas Athene
Rose, like a pillar of tall white cloud, toward silver
    Olympus;
Far above ocean and shore, and the peaks of the isles
    and the mainland,
Where no frost nor storm is, in clear blue windless
    abysses,

High in the home of the summer, the seats of the happy
  Immortals.

In spite of its rarity (or perhaps because of it) the spondaic
hexameter, that is one with a spondee in the fifth foot, was often
affected by Catullus and his circle, and at LXIV 78 Catullus has
three in a row.

  $\underline{\prime} \cup \cup \quad \underline{\prime} \cup \cup \quad \underline{\prime} \cup \cup \quad \underline{\prime} \cup \cup \quad \underline{\prime} - \quad \underline{\prime} -$

  Thence he will follow the Indian trails to the Ozark
    Mountains.

Either or both of the first two dactyls in the pentameter may be
replaced by spondees, a substitution never found in the second
half of the verse.

  $\underline{\prime} - \quad \underline{\prime} - \quad \underline{\prime} \parallel \underline{\prime} \cup \cup \quad \underline{\prime} \cup \cup \quad \underline{\prime}$

  All day pale blue smoke rose from a hundred abodes.

Some verses of Longfellow's (containing, it must be noted, a few
metrical licences) will assist in inculcating the rhythm of the
elegiac couplet.

  Dark is the morning with mist; in the narrow mouth of the
    harbour
  Motionless lies the sea, under its curtain of cloud;
  Dreamily glimmer the sails of the ships on the distant
    horizon,
    Like to the towers of a town, built on the verge of the
      sea.
  Slowly and stately and still, they sail forth into the ocean;
    With them sail my thoughts over the limitless deep.
  Farther and farther away, borne on by unsatisfied longings,
    Unto Hesperian isles, unto Ausonian shores.

CATULLUS

edited from the primary manuscripts

*Versus domini Benevenuti de Campexanis de Vincencia
de resurrectione Catulli poetae Veronensis*

Ad patriam venio longis a finibus exul;
  causa mei reditus compatriota fuit,
scilicet a calamis tribuit cui Francia nomen
  quique notat turbae praetereuntis iter.
quo licet ingenio vestrum celebrate Catullum,
  cujus sub modio clausa papyrus erat.

*Verses of Benvenuto Campesani of Vicenza on the
reappearance of the Veronese poet Catullus*

I come back from exile in a distant land:
  a fellow citizen was the cause of my return,
he in fact whom France has given a name from reeds
  and who watches the path of the passing crowd.
With what appreciation ye may, enjoy your Catullus,
  whose book lay hidden under a bushel.

Incipit Catulli Veronensis Liber

I

Cui dono lepidum novum libellum
arido modo pumice expolitum?
Corneli, tibi: namque tu solebas
meas esse aliquid putare nugas
jam tum, cum ausus es unus Italorum   5
omne aevum tribus explicare chartis,
doctis, Juppiter, et laboriosis.
quare habe tibi quidquid hoc libelli,
qualecumque quidem patroni ut ergo
plus uno maneat perenne saeclo.   10

Here begins the Book of Catullus of Verona

Dedication to Cornelius Nepos

To whom do I give my pretty new book,
freshly polished with dry pumice?
To you, Cornelius, for already you used to
consider my nothings of some value
when you, the only Italian to dare to do so,
unfolded the whole of history in three rolls,
learned ones, by Jove, and full of labour, too.
Wherefore accept this trifle of a book,
however slight, that thanks to its patron it may
live on through the years for many an age to come.

II

Passer, deliciae meae puellae,
quicum ludere, quem in sinu tenere,
cui primum digitum dare appetenti
et acres solet incitare morsus
cum desiderio meo nitenti   5
carum nescioquid libet jocari,
credo, ut, cum gravis acquiescet ardor,   8
sit solaciolum sui doloris: 7
tecum ludere, sicut ipsa, posse
et tristes animi levare curas   10
tam gratumst mihi quam ferunt puellae
pernici aureolum fuisse malum,
quod zonam soluit diu ligatam.

III

Lugete, o Veneres Cupidinesque,
et quantumst hominum venustiorum!
passer mortuus est meae puellae,
passer, deliciae meae puellae,
quem plus illa oculis suis amabat: 5
nam mellitus erat suamque norat
ipsam tam bene quam puella matrem,
nec sese a gremio illius movebat,
sed circumsiliens modo huc modo illuc
ad solam dominam usque pipiabat.   10
qui nunc it per iter tenebricosum
illuc, unde negant redire quemquam.
at vobis male sit, malae tenebrae
Orci, quae omnia bella devoratis:
tam bellum mihi passerem abstulistis.   15
o factum male, quod, miselle passer,
tua nunc opera meae puellae
flendo turgiduli rubent ocelli!

Lesbia's sparrow

O sparrow that are my sweetheart's pet,
with whom she likes to play, whom to hold in her lap,
to whose pecking to offer her finger-tips
and provoke you to bite sharply
whenever it pleases her, bright-eyed with longing for me,
to engage in some endearing frolic
so that, I fancy, when her fierce passion subsides,
it may prove a diversion for her pain:
to be able to play with you, as does your mistress,
and allay the sad cares of my heart
would be as welcome to me as they say
was to the swift-footed girl that golden apple
which loosed her long-tied girdle.

The sparrow dies

Mourn, you Venuses and Cupids,
and all the lovers that there are!
My sweetheart's sparrow is dead,
the sparrow that was my sweetheart's pet,
which she loved more than her own eyes:
for it was honey-sweet, and knew its
mistress as well as a girl knows her own mother,
nor would it stir from her lap,
but hopping about, now here, now there,
would ever chirp for its mistress alone.
But now it travels along a darkling path
to a place from which they say no one returns.
A curse upon you, accursed darkness
of Orcus, that consumes all pretty things:
such a pretty sparrow you have robbed me of.
Ah cruel event, that through your doing,
hapless sparrow, my sweetheart's eyes
are red and swollen with weeping!

IV

Phaselus ille, quem videtis, hospites,
ait fuisse navium celerrimus,
neque ullius natantis impetum trabis
nequisse praeterire, sive palmulis
opus foret volare sive linteo.　　　　　　　　　5
et hoc negat minacis Hadriatici
negare litus insulasve Cycladas
Rhodumque nobilem horridamque Thracia
Propontida trucemve Ponticum sinum,
ubi iste post phaselus antea fuit　　　　　　　10
comata silva: nam Cytorio in jugo
loquente saepe sibilum edidit coma.

Amastri Pontica et Cytore buxifer,
tibi haec fuisse et esse cognitissima
ait phaselus; ultima ex origine　　　　　　　15
tuo stetisse dicit in cacumine,
tuo imbuisse palmulas in aequore,
et inde tot per impotentia freta
erum tulisse, laeva sive dextera
vocaret aura, sive utrumque Juppiter　　　　　20
simul secundus incidisset in pedem;
neque ulla vota litoralibus deis
sibi esse facta, cum veniret a mari
novissime hunc ad usque limpidum lacum.

sed haec prius fuere: nunc recondita　　　　　25
senet quiete seque dedicat tibi,
gemelle Castor et gemelle Castoris.

On his yacht

That yacht which you see, my friends,
says that it was the swiftest of ships
and never failed to outstrip the dash
of any craft afloat, whether there was
need to wing her way with oar or sail;
and she says this is not gainsaid by the coast of
the angry Adriatic or the Cyclades or famous Rhodes
or the Propontis ruffled by the offshore wind
from Thrace or the savage Pontic gulf,
where the yacht-to-be was earlier
a leafy wood: for many a day on the heights of Cytorus
she sent forth whispers from her vocal foliage.

Pontic Amastris and Cytorus clad with box,
the yacht says that this was and is
well known to you; she says that from her
remotest origin she stood upon your summit,
first in your waters dipped her oars,
and thence over so many raging seas
carried her master, whether the breeze piped from port
or starboard, or a favouring wind from Jove
came down upon both sheets at once;
nor had any vows to the gods of the shore
been made on her behalf when at the last she made her way
from the sea right up to this crystal lake.

But these things belong to the past: now she grows old
in peaceful retirement and dedicates herself to you,
twin Castor and Castor's twin.

V

Vivamus, mea Lesbia, atque amemus,
rumoresque senum severiorum
omnes unius aestimemus assis.
soles occidere et redire possunt:
nobis, cum semel occidit brevis lux,   5
nox est perpetua una dormienda.
da mi basia mille, deinde centum,
dein mille altera, dein secunda centum,
deinde usque altera mille, deinde centum.
dein, cum milia multa fecerimus,   10
conturbabimus illa, ne sciamus,
aut nequis malus invidere possit,
cum tantum sciat esse basiorum.

Kisses for Catullus

Let us live, my Lesbia, and love,
and value at one penny all
the talk of stern old men.
Suns can set and rise again:
we, when once our brief light has set,
must sleep one never-ending night.
Give me a thousand kisses, then a hundred,
then a second thousand, then a second hundred,
then yet another thousand, then a hundred.
Then, when we have made up many thousands,
we will wreck the count, lest we know it
or any devil have power to cast an evil eye upon us
when he knows the total of our kisses.

VI

Flavi, delicias tuas Catullo,
ni sint illepidae atque inelegantes,
velles dicere nec tacere posses.
verum nescioquid febriculosi
scorti diligis: hoc pudet fateri.   5
nam te non viduas jacere noctes
nequiquam tacitum cubile clamat
sertis ac Syrio fragrans olivo,
pulvinusque peraeque et hic et ille
attritus, tremulique quassa lecti   10
argutatio inambulatioque.
nil perstare valet, nihil tacere.
cur? non tam latera effututa pandas,
ni tu quid facias ineptiarum.
quare, quidquid habes boni malique,   15
dic nobis: volo te ac tuos amores
ad caelum lepido vocare versu.

VII

Quaeris, quot mihi basiationes
tuae, Lesbia, sint satis superque.
quam magnus numerus Libyssae harenae
laserpiciferis jacet Cyrenis,
oraclum Jovis inter aestuosi   5
et Batti veteris sacrum sepulcrum;
aut quam sidera multa, cum tacet nox,
furtivos hominum vident amores:
tam te basia multa basiare
vesano satis et super Catullost,   10
quae nec pernumerare curiosi
possint nec mala fascinare lingua.

A clandestine affair

Flavius, if your new girl-friend were not devoid
of wit and charm, you would want to tell
Catullus about her and be unable to stop talking.
You must be keen on some pasty-faced
bit of skirt and ashamed to admit it.
For that you are not spending nights on your own
the bed, whose silence is futile, simply shouts aloud,
perfumed as it is with garlands and exotic scents,
as do the dents right and left on the bolster,
and the chattering and shuffling
of the rickety bed when shaken.
It's no use standing fast in denial, no use being silent.
You ask why? Well, you wouldn't present such a debauched
sight unless you were up to some fancy capers.
Therefore, whatever you are hiding, fair or foul,
out with it! I want to proclaim you and your love
to the skies in witty verse.

Kisses for Lesbia

You ask, Lesbia, how many kissings
of you are enough and to spare for me.
As great the number of the sands of Libya
to be found in silphium-bearing Cyrene
between Jove's torrid oracle
and the sacred tomb of legendary Battus;
or as many the stars which in the silence of night
behold the stealthy loves of mankind:
so many kisses to kiss you with
would be enough and to spare for love-crazed Catullus,
too many for the inquisitive to be able to count
or bewitch with their evil tongues.

VIII

Miser Catulle, desinas ineptire,
et quod vides perisse perditum ducas.
fulsere quondam candidi tibi soles,
cum ventitabas quo puella ducebat,
amata nobis quantum amabitur nulla.   5
ibi illa multa tum jocosa fiebant,
quae tu volebas nec puella nolebat.
fulsere vere candidi tibi soles.
nunc jam illa non vult: tu quoque, impotens, noli,
nec quae fugit sectare, nec miser vive,   10
sed obstinata mente perfer, obdura.
vale, puella, jam Catullus obdurat,
nec te requiret nec rogabit invitam.
at tu dolebis, cum rogaberis nulla.
scelesta, vae te! quae tibi manet vita?   15
quis nunc te adibit? cui videberis bella?
quem nunc amabis? cujus esse diceris?
quem basiabis? cui labella mordebis?
at tu, Catulle, destinatus obdura!

IX

Verani, omnibus e meis amicis
antistans mihi milibus trecentis,
venistine domum ad tuos penates
fratresque unanimos anumque matrem?
venisti. o mihi nuntii beati!   5
visam te incolumem audiamque Hiberum
narrantem loca, facta, nationes,
ut mos est tuus, applicansque collum
jucundum os oculosque saviabor.
o quantumst hominum beatiorum,   10
quid me laetius est beatiusve?

Disillusionment

Poor Catullus, you must stop being silly,
and count as lost what you see is lost.
Once the sun shone bright for you,
when you would go whither your sweetheart led,
she you loved as no woman will ever be loved again.
Then there took place those many jolly scenes
which you desired nor did your sweetheart not desire.
Truly the sun shone bright for you.
Now she desires no more: do you too, weakling, not desire;
and do not chase her who flees, nor live in unhappiness,
but harden your heart, endure, and stand fast.
Goodbye, sweetheart. Catullus now stands fast:
he will not look for you or court you against your will.
But you will be sorry when you are not courted at all.
Wretch, pity on you! What life lies in store for you!
Who will come to you now? Who will think you pretty?
Whom will you love now? Whose will people say you are?
Whom will you kiss? Whose lips will you bite?
But you, Catullus, be resolute and stand fast.

A welcome home to his friend

Veranius, you who of all my friends
are worth more in my eyes than a million,
have you really returned to your hearth and home,
to loving brothers and aged mother?
Yes, you have. O happy news for me!
I shall see you safe and sound, and hear you telling
in your own inimitable way of the sights and scenes
and tribes of Spain, and drawing your head
towards me I shall kiss your sweet lips and eyes.
Of all the happy people in the world
what man is gladder or happier than I?

X

Varus me meus ad suos amores
visum duxerat e foro otiosum,
scortillum, ut mihi tum repente visumst,
non sane illepidum neque invenustum.
huc ut venimus, incidere nobis   5
sermones varii, in quibus, quid esset
jam Bithynia, quo modo se haberet,
ecquonam mihi profuisset aere.
respondi, id quod erat, nihil neque ipsis
nunc praetoribus esse nec cohorti,   10
cur quisquam caput unctius referret,
praesertim quibus esset irrumator
praetor, nec faceret pili cohortem.
'at certe tamen,' inquiunt 'quod illic
natum dicitur esse, comparasti   15
ad lecticam homines.' ego, ut puellae
unum me facerem beatiorem,
'non' inquam 'mihi tam fuit maligne,
ut, provincia quod mala incidisset,
non possem octo homines parare rectos.'   20
at mi nullus erat nec hic neque illic,
fractum qui veteris pedem grabati
in collo sibi collocare posset.
hic illa, ut decuit cinaediorem,
'quaeso,' inquit mihi 'mi Catulle, paulum   25
istos commoda! nam volo ad Serapim
deferri.' 'mane,' inquii puellae,
'istud quod modo dixeram me habere,
fugit me ratio: meus sodalis,
Cinnast Gaius, is sibi paravit.   30
verum, utrum illius an mei, quid ad me?
utor tam bene quam mihi paratis.
sed tu insula male et molesta vivis,
per quam non licet esse neglegentem.'

Caught out in a fib

While I was idling in the forum, my friend Varus
took me off to meet his girl-friend,
a proper tart, as I realized at once,
though not without wit or charm.
When we got there, various topics
of conversation came up, including
Bithynia today, what state it was in,
and how much money I had made out of it.
I told them, as was the truth, that nowadays
neither praetors themselves nor their staff
have any means of feathering their nests,
especially those who had a sod of a praetor
over them, who didn't give a damn for his staff.
'Nevertheless,' they say 'you surely
acquired some litter-bearers, said to be
a local product.' Said I, to make myself
specially privileged in the eyes of the girl,
'I didn't do so badly,
in spite of being saddled with a bad province,
as not to acquire eight sturdy men.'
The truth was that I hadn't a single man,
here or there, to put on his back
the broken leg of a run-down sofa.
At this the girl, as befitted the hussy she was,
says to me: 'Please, Catullus, do just lend
them for a bit, for I want to be carried
to Serapis's.' 'Wait,' say I to the girl
'what I just now said I had,
I wasn't thinking: it's my friend—
Gaius Cinna that is—it's he who bought them.
But whether his or mine, what's that to me?
I use them just like what I've bought myself.
But you are damned awkward and a nuisance
not to let a fellow make a slip of the tongue.'

XI

Furi et Aureli, comites Catulli,
sive in extremos penetrabit Indos,
litus ut longe resonante Eoa
    tunditur unda,

sive in Hyrcanos Arabasve molles,   5
seu Sacas sagittiferosve Parthos,
sive quae septemgeminus colorat
    aequora Nilus,

sive trans altas gradietur Alpes,
Caesaris visens monumenta magni,   10
Gallicum Rhenum, horribiles quoque ulti-
    mosque Britannos,

omnia haec, quaecumque feret voluntas
caelitum, temptare simul parati:
pauca nuntiate meae puellae   15
    non bona dicta.

cum suis vivat valeatque moechis,
quos simul complexa tenet trecentos,
nullum amans vere, sed identidem omnium
    ilia rumpens;   20

nec meum respectet, ut ante, amorem,
qui illius culpa cecidit velut prati
ultimi flos, praetereunte postquam
    tactus aratrost.

Last message to Lesbia

Furius and Aurelius, ready to accompany Catullus,
whether he plans to penetrate to the distant Indians,
where the shore is pounded by the far-resounding
    wave of the orient

or to the Hyrcani and the luxurious Arabs
or the Sacae and the quivered Parthians
or the plains that are dyed by the flooding of
    the sevenfold Nile,

or whether he plans to march over the mountainous Alps,
viewing the places that tell of mighty Caesar,
the Gallic Rhine, and also the horrible Britons
    at the world's end—

ready as you are to face all these hazards with me,
whatever the will of heaven above will bring:
take back to my sweetheart a brief
    and not kind message.

Let her live and be happy with her lovers,
three-hundred of whom at once she holds in her embraces,
loving none truly but again and again rupturing
    the loins of them all;

and let her not count on my love, as in the past,
for through her fault it has fallen like a flower
at the meadow's edge, after being lopped
    by the passing plough.

XII

Marrucine Asini, manu sinistra
non belle uteris in joco atque vino:
tollis lintea neglegentiorum.
hoc salsum esse putas? fugit te, inepte:
quamvis sordida res et invenustast.   5
non credis mihi? crede Pollioni
fratri, qui tua furta vel talento
mutari velit: est enim leporum
differtus puer ac facetiarum.
quare aut hendecasyllabos trecentos   10
exspecta, aut mihi linteum remitte;
quod me non movet aestimatione,
verumst mnemosynum mei sodalis.
nam sudaria Saetaba ex Hiberis
miserunt mihi muneri Fabullus   15
et Veranius: haec amem necessest
ut Veraniolum meum et Fabullum.

XIII

Cenabis bene, mi Fabulle, apud me
paucis, si tibi di favent, diebus,
si tecum attuleris bonam atque magnam
cenam, non sine candida puella
et vino et sale et omnibus cachinnis.   5
haec si, inquam, attuleris, venuste noster,
cenabis bene: nam tui Catulli
plenus sacculus est aranearum.
sed contra accipies meros amores
seu quid suavius elegantiusvest: 10
nam unguentum dabo, quod meae puellae
donarunt Veneres Cupidinesque;
quod tu cum olfacies, deos rogabis,
totum ut te faciant, Fabulle, nasum.

To a light-fingered acquaintance

Marrucinian Asinius, it isn't a nice use you make
of your left hand while we are jesting and drinking:
you steal the napkins of any off their guard.
D'you think this funny? You've got it wrong, idiot!
It's no end of a mean and revolting trick.
You don't believe me? Then believe your brother
Pollio, who would give as much as a talent
to have your thefts undone: for he really is a lad
brimful of wit and pleasantry.
So either be prepared for reams
of lampoons, or send me back my napkin.
It isn't its value that troubles me,
but it is a souvenir of friends of mine.
For Fabullus and Veranius sent me
Saetaban napkins from Spain
as a gift: and I cannot help treasuring them
as much as I do my dear Veranius and Fabullus.

Invitation to dinner

Yes, Fabullus, you'll dine in style at my place
one day soon, if the gods smile on you,
if you bring with you a nice big
dinner, not forgetting a pretty girl
and wine and wit and everything to make us laugh.
If, I say, you bring all this, my dear fellow,
you will dine in style: for the purse of
your Catullus is full of—cobwebs.
Still, in return you'll get the very essence of love
or something still more fragrant and exquisite,
if something there be: for I will give you a perfume
that the Venuses and Cupids gave to my sweetheart;
once you smell it, you'll ask the gods,
Fabullus, to make you all nose.

XIV A

Ni te plus oculis meis amarem,
jucundissime Calve, munere isto
odissem te odio Vatiniano:
nam quid feci ego quidve sum locutus,
cur me tot male perderes poetis?   5
isti di mala multa dent clienti,
qui tantum tibi misit impiorum.
quod si, ut suspicor, hoc novum ac repertum
munus dat tibi Sulla litterator,
non est mi male, sed bene ac beate,   10
quod non dispereunt tui labores.
di magni, horribilem et sacrum libellum!
quem tu scilicet ad tuum Catullum
misti, continuo ut die periret,
Saturnalibus, optimo dierum!   15
non non hoc tibi, salse, sic abibit:
nam, si luxerit, ad librariorum
curram scrinia; Caesios, Aquinos,
Suffenum, omnia colligam venena,
ac te his suppliciis remunerabor.   20
vos hinc interea valete abite
illuc, unde malum pedem attulistis,
saecli incommoda, pessimi poetae!

A humorous Christmas present

Did I not love you more than my eyes,
most genial Calvus, I should for that present of yours
hate you with all the hatred that Vatinius bears you:
for what have I done, what have I said, that you
should poison me with such a dose of poets?
May the gods heap evils on that client
who sent you such a god-forsaken crew.
But if, as I suspect, this new and exquisite
offering is a gift to you from the schoolteacher Sulla,
I am not displeased, but happy and delighted
that your labours were not spent in vain.
Great gods, what an awful and abominable book!
And you of course had to send it to your Catullus
to kill him off on the following day,
on the Saturnalia, the happiest of days!
No, no, you joker, you won't get away with it scot-free.
For, come the dawn, I shall run down
to the booksellers' stalls and collect your Caesii,
your Aquini, Suffenus, and all such poisonous trash,
and with these torments repay you in kind.
Goodbye to you meanwhile, and hence begone
to where you brought your atrocious feet from,
pests of the age, you execrable poets!

XIV B

Siqui forte mearum ineptiarum
lectores eritis manusque vestras
non horrebitis admovere nobis,
omnem ponite nunc severitatem:
nam versus veniunt proterviores.

XV

Commendo tibi me ac meos amores,
Aureli. veniam peto pudenter,
ut, si quicquam animo tuo cupisti,
quod castum expeteres et integellum,
conserves puerum mihi pudice,   5
non dico a populo—nihil veremur
istos, qui in platea modo huc modo illuc
in re praetereunt sua occupati—
verum a te metuo tuoque pene
infesto pueris bonis malisque.   10
quem tu qua libet, ut libet, moveto
quantum vis, ubi erit foris paratum:
hunc unum excipio, ut puto, pudenter.
quod si te mala mens furorque vecors
in tantam impulerit, sceleste, culpam,   15
ut nostrum insidiis caput lacessas,
ah tum te miserum malique fati,
quem attractis pedibus patente porta
percurrent raphanique mugilesque!

Announcing a chapter of risqué poems

If perchance you readers
of my trifles do not shrink
from fingering my pages,
now lay aside all inhibition, for verses
follow which are rather daring.

Hands off my boy!

I am putting myself and my loved one in your hands,
Aurelius. I humbly ask a favour:
if you've ever desired with all your heart
to keep something chaste and innocent,
please preserve my boy in decency,
I don't mean from common folk, for I don't fear
anything from the people who go to and fro in the
streets absorbed in their own business:
it's you and your penis I'm afraid of,
ready to attack good boys and bad alike.
Set it in motion to your heart's content where and
how you please, when you get a chance abroad.
But this one boy I ask you (humbly, I think) to spare.
But if infatuation and frantic lust
drive you, you villain, to the awful crime
of setting a snare for me,
then I pity you for your sorry fate,
for with feet pulled up and your backdoor wide open
you'll suffer the thrust of radishes and mullets.

XVI

Pedicabo ego vos et irrumabo,
Aureli pathice et cinaede Furi,
qui me ex versiculis meis putastis,
quod sunt molliculi, parum pudicum.
nam castum esse decet pium poetam   5
ipsum, versiculos nihil necessest;
qui tum denique habent salem ac leporem,
si sunt molliculi ac parum pudici
et quod pruriat incitare possunt,
non dico pueris, sed his pilosis,   10
qui duros nequeunt movere lumbos.
vos, quod milia multa basiorum
legistis, male me marem putatis?
pedicabo ego vos et irrumabo.

In defence of his decency

Bugger you and stuff you,
you catamite Aurelius and you pervert Furius,
who think me immodest
because my verses are rather naughty.
For the dedicated poet has to be decent,
though there's no need for his verses to be so.
Why, they only acquire wit and spice
if they are rather naughty and immodest,
and can rouse with their ticklings,
I don't mean boys, but those hairy old 'uns
unable to stir their arthritic loins.
Because you've read of my many thousand
kisses, do you think I'm less virile on that account?
Yes, I'll bugger you and stuff you all right!

XVII

O colonia, quae cupis
    ponte ludere longo,
et salire paratum habes,
    sed vereris inepta
crura ponticuli axiclis
    stantis in recidivis,
ne supinus eat cavaque
    in palude recumbat:
sic tibi bonus ex tua
    pons libidine fiat,   5
in quo vel Salisubsili
    sacra suscipiantur,
munus hoc mihi maximi
    da, colonia, risus.
quendam municipem meum
    de tuo volo ponte
ire praecipitem in lutum
    per caputque pedesque,
verum totius ut lacus
    putidaeque paludis   10
lividissima maximeque
    est profunda vorago.
insulsissimus est homo,
    nec sapit pueri instar
bimuli tremula patris
    dormientis in ulna.

A stupid husband

O Colony, who wish to have
   a long bridge to play games on,
and are ready to dance,
   but fear the shaky legs
that prop up the poor old bridge
   on tottering supports,
in case it falls on its back and
   finds a bed in the depths of the swamp:
on one condition may you get a bridge
   good enough to satisfy your heart's desire,
on which even the rites of the leap-frogging
   god may be undertaken—
that you grant me, Colony, this gift
   to make me laugh my loudest.
There is a certain fellow-townsman of mine
   I want to see tumble headlong
into the mud from your bridge
   head over heels:
only let it be where the whole marsh
   and stinking swamp
provides the blackest
   and deepest abyss.
The fellow is a perfect idiot,
   and has not as much sense as a child
two years old rocked asleep
   in the arms of its father.

cui cum sit viridissimo
    nupta flore puella
(et puella tenellulo
    delicatior haedo,   15
asservanda nigerrimis
    diligentius uvis),
ludere hanc sinit ut libet,
    nec pili facit uni,
nec se sublevat ex sua
    parte, sed velut alnus
in fossa Liguri jacet
    suppernata securi,
tantundem omnia sentiens
    quam si nulla sit usquam;   20
talis iste merus stupor
    nil videt, nihil audit,
ipse qui sit, utrum sit an
    non sit, id quoque nescit..
nunc eum volo de tuo
    ponte mittere pronum,
si pote stolidum repente
    excitare veternum,
et supinum animum in gravi
    derelinquere caeno,   25
ferream ut soleam tenaci
    in voragine mula.

Though he has for wife a girl
   in the freshest flower of youth,
(a girl, too, more skittish
   than a tender kidling,
who ought to be guarded
   more carefully than the ripest grapes),
he lets her play as she wishes,
   and cares not a straw
nor rouses himself for his part,
   but lies like an alder
in a ditch hamstrung
   by a Ligurian axe,
as little awake to everything
   as though it did not exist at all.
Such is that perfect idiot:
   he sees nothing, he hears nothing;
and who he is, whether he is or
   is not, this too he knows not.
Now I want to send him
   headlong from your bridge,
in case he can suddenly
   startle his stupid lethargy
and leave his sluggish spirit
   behind in the boggy mire,
as a mule her iron shoe
   in the clinging mud.

XXI

Aureli, pater esuritionum,
non harum modo, sed quot aut fuerunt
aut sunt aut aliis erunt in annis,
pedicare cupis meos amores.
nec clam: nam simul es, jocaris una,   5
haerens ad latus omnia experiris.
frustra: nam insidias mihi struentem
tangam te prior irrumatione.
atque id si faceres satur, tacerem:
nunc ipsum id doleo, quod esurire   10
a temet puer et sitire discet.
quare desine, dum licet pudico,
ne finem facias, sed irrumatus.

Stop it, Aurelius!

Aurelius, father of famines,
not just of these, but of all that were
or are or will be in years to come,
you wish to bugger my boy. And not on the quiet:
for you're always with him, always laughing with him,
and fussing over him you leave nothing untried.
It's no good: for though you plot against me,
I'll get in first and stuff you.
If you did it on a full stomach, I'd keep quiet:
as it is, I'm vexed that the boy is going
to learn from you to starve and thirst.
So stop it, while you decently can,
or else you'll finish by getting stuffed.

XXII

Suffenus iste, Vare, quem probe nosti,
homost venustus et dicax et urbanus,
idemque longe plurimos facit versus.
puto esse ego illi milia aut decem aut plura
perscripta, nec sic ut fit in palimpsesto   5
relata: chartae regiae novae bibli,
novi umbilici, lora rubra membranae—
derecta plumbo et pumice omnia aequata.
haec cum legas, tum bellus ille et urbanus
Suffenus unus caprimulgus aut fossor   10
rursus videtur: tantum abhorret ac mutat.
hoc quid putamus esse? qui modo scurra
aut siquid hac re scitius videbatur,
idem inficetost inficetior rure,
simul poemata attigit, neque idem umquam   15
aequest beatus ac poema cum scribit:
tam gaudet in se tamque se ipse miratur.
nimirum idem omnes fallimur, nequest quisquam,
quem non in aliqua re videre Suffenum
possis. suus cuique attributus est error: 20
sed non videmus manticae quod in tergost.

A good fellow but a bad poet

That Suffenus, Varus, whom you know so well,
is a man who is charming and witty and elegant
and also composes far more verses than anyone else.
I think he has written ten thousand or more,
and not, as people do, scribbled them on paper
used before: imperial sheets of new papyrus,
new bosses, red straps for the wrapper,
everything ruled with lead and smoothed with pumice.
When you read his verses, the smart and elegant
Suffenus now seems a mere goatherd
or ditch-digger: he is so unlike himself and changed.
What are we to think of this? He who just now
seemed a polished wit or smarter even than that,
is at the same time clumsier than the clumsy country
as soon as he touches poetry, and yet he is never
so happy as when he is writing a poem:
so delighted is he with himself and so admires his skill.
Of course we all share the same delusion, and no one
is not seen to be in some respect a Suffenus.
Everyone has assigned to him his own failing; but we do not
see the part of the bag which hangs on our back.

XXIII

Furi, cui neque servus est neque arca
nec cimex neque araneus neque ignis,
verum est et pater et noverca, quorum
dentes vel silicem comesse possunt,
est pulchre tibi cum tuo parente   5
et cum conjuge lignea parentis.
nec mirum: bene nam valetis omnes,
pulchre concoquitis, nihil timetis,
non incendia, non graves ruinas,
non facta impia, non dolos veneni,   10
non casus alios periculorum.
atqui corpora sicciora cornu
aut siquid magis aridumst habetis
sole et frigore et esuritione.
quare non tibi sit bene ac beate?   15
a te sudor abest, abest saliva,
mucusque et mala pituita nasi.
hanc ad munditiem adde mundiorem,
quod culus tibi purior salillost,
nec toto decies cacas in anno;   20
atque id durius est faba et lupillis,
quod tu si manibus teras fricesque,
non umquam digitum inquinare possis.
haec tu commoda tam beata, Furi,
noli spernere nec putare parvi,   25
et sestertia quae soles precari
centum desine: nam sat es beatus.

Count your blessings, Furius

Furius, who haven't slave or purse
or bug or spider or fire,
but do have a father and a stepmother, whose
teeth can chew even flint,
a fine time you have with your father
and the scraggy wife of your father.
No wonder: for you all enjoy good health,
have fine digestions, and have nothing to be afraid of—
no fires, no disastrous house-collapses,
no criminal assaults, no plots to poison you, and
no other dangerous occurrences.
Moreover, what with sun and cold and fasting,
you have bodies as dry as bone
or drier still if drier thing there be.
Why should you not be comfortable and well?
You are free from sweat and slobber,
from catarrh and an annoying runny nose.
Add to this cleanliness one still cleaner
in that your backside is shinier than a salt-cellar,
for you shit less than ten times a year;
and then you produce something harder than beans or lupins,
which if you were to rub and crumble in your hands,
you'd never be able to dirty a finger.
Having such fine blessings as these, Furius,
do not despise them or think little of them,
and stop your constant begging
for a hundred grand: you are well enough off already.

XXIV

O qui flosculus es Juventiorum,
non horum modo, sed quot aut fuerunt
aut posthac aliis erunt in annis,
mallem divitias Midae dedisses
isti, cui neque servus est neque arca,   5
quam sic te sineres ab illo amari.
'quid? non est homo bellus?' inquies. est:
sed bello huic neque servus est neque arca.
hoc tu quam libet abice elevaque:
nec servum tamen ille habet neque arcam.   10

XXV

Cinaede Thalle, mollior cuniculi capillo
vel anseris medullula vel imula oricilla
vel pene languido senis situque araneoso,
idemque, Thalle, turbida rapacior procella,
cum dives arca rimulas ostendit oscitantes,   5
remitte pallium mihi meum, quod involasti,
sudariumque Saetabum catagraphosque Thynos,
inepte, quae palam soles habere tamquam avita.
quae nunc tuis ab unguibus reglutina et remitte,
ne laneum latusculum manusque mollicellas   10
inusta turpiter tibi conscribilent flagella,
et insolenter aestues, velut minuta magno
deprensa navis in mari, vesaniente vento.

XXVI

Furi, villula vestra non ad Austri
flatus oppositast neque ad Favoni
nec saevi Boreae aut Apheliotae,
verum ad milia quindecim et ducentos.
o ventum horribilem atque pestilentem!   5

Rebuke to Juventius

O you who are the flower of the Juventii,
not just of these, but all that have been
or will hereafter be in years to come,
I wish rather that you had bestowed all Midas' wealth
on him who has neither slave nor purse
than thus allow yourself to be wooed by him.
'What? Isn't he a fine fellow?' you ask. He is:
but this fine fellow has neither slave nor purse.
You may discuss and disparage this for all you're worth:
he'll still have neither slave nor purse.

To another light-fingered friend

Pansy Thallus, softer than rabbit's fur
or goose's nicest down or lobe of tender ear
or dotard's drooping dinky and its spiderwebs,
yet also, Thallus, more rapacious than a violent hurricane
when a well-stocked linen-chest has openings showing,
send back my cloak that you've pounced upon
and my Spanish napkin and Bithynian printed towels,
which, idiot, you keep on parading as heirlooms.
Just unglue them from your claws and send them back,
or your flabby little flanks and your tender little hands
will be scribbled all over by base brandings of the lash,
and you'll pitch and toss as never before, like a little
boat caught on the mighty sea in a tempestuous gale.

A horrible draught

Furius, that country-house of yours has not been put up
against the blasts of the South Wind or the West
or the bitter North or the East, but against a mortgage
of fifteen-thousand and two-hundred sesterces.
Oh what a horrible dangerous draught!

XXVII

Minister vetuli puer Falerni,
inger mi calices amariores,
ut lex Postumiae jubet magistrae
ebrioso acino ebriosioris.
at vos quo libet hinc abite, lymphae,   5
vini pernicies, et ad severos
migrate: hic merus est Thyonianus.

XXVIII

Pisonis comites, cohors inanis,
aptis sarcinulis et expeditis,
Verani optime tuque mi Fabulle,
quid rerum geritis? satisne cum isto
vappa frigoraque et famen tulistis?   5
ecquidnam in tabulis patet lucelli
expensum, ut mihi, qui meum secutus
praetorem refero datum lucello?
o Memmi, bene me ac diu supinum
tota ista trabe lentus irrumasti.   10
sed, quantum video, pari fuistis
casu: nam nihilo minore verpa
farti estis. pete nobiles amicos!
at vobis mala multa di deaeque
dent, opprobria Romuli Remique.   15

Prefacing poems of stronger stuff

Young steward of old Falernian wine,
pour me out cups of stronger stuff, as bids
the decree of Postumia, mistress of the feast,
who's tipsier than the tipsy grape.
But you, water, anywhere it please you hence begone,
you ruination of wine, and be off to the sober:
this man is an unqualified devotee of Bacchus.

The scant rewards of foreign service

You aides of Piso, needy entourage
with trim little packs that are easy to carry,
excellent Veranius and you, dear Fabullus,
how are you getting on? Have you suffered enough
cold and hunger under that wash-out?
Do profits show in your account-books
on the wrong side, as with me, who in service with
my governor reckon my outgoings as profit?
Yes, Memmius, well and truly did you get me on my back
and calmly stuff me with the whole length of your beam!
Yet, as far as I can see, you two are in
like case: for you have been filled with no less
a poker. So much for running after noble friends!
But may the gods and goddesses heap curses on the pair
of you, you blots on the names of Romulus and Remus!

XXIX

Quis hoc potest videre, quis potest pati,
nisi impudicus et vorax et aleo,
Mamurram habere quod comata Gallia
habebat ante et ultima Britannia?
cinaede Romule, hoc videbis et feres?   5
et ille nunc superbus et superfluens
perambulabit omnium cubilia,
ut albulus columbus aut Adoneus?
cinaede Romule, hoc videbis et feres?
es impudicus et vorax et aleo.   10

eone nomine, imperator unice,
fuisti in ultima occidentis insula,
ut ista vestra diffututa mentula
ducenties comesset aut trecenties?
quid est alid sinistra liberalitas?   15
parum expatravit an parum helluatus est?
paterna prima lancinata sunt bona,
secunda praeda Pontica, inde tertia
Hibera, quam scit amnis aurifer Tagus.
eine Galliae optima et Britanniae?   20

quid hunc, malum, fovetis? aut quid hic potest
nisi uncta devorare patrimonia?
eone nomine, urbis o piissimi,
socer generque, perdidistis omnia?

Indignation with Mamurra

Who can see this, who can stand this,
unless lost to shame and a glutton and a gambler,
Mamurra in possession of what long-haired Gaul
and farthest Britain once possessed?
Pansy Romulus, can you see and stand this?
And is he now, overbearing and overwealthy,
to prance around everyone's marriage-bed,
like a lily-white dove or the god Adonis?
Pansy Romulus, can you see and stand this?
Then you're lost to shame and a glutton and a gambler.

Was it on this account, O general without peer,
that you found yourself in the farthest island of the west,
in order that that debauched tool of yours
might get through twenty or thirty million?
What is misplaced generosity if not this?
Hasn't he lechered away enough or wasted enough on gluttony?
First his patrimony was dissipated,
then his Pontic loot, and thirdly
that from Spain, of which the gold-bearing Tagus can tell.
Is this the man who has the pickings of Gaul and Britain?

Why the devil do you pamper him, the two of you?
And what can he do except swallow tidy fortunes?
Was it on this account, most honourable men of Rome,
father- and son-in-law, that you ruined the world?

XXX

Alfene immemor atque unanimis false sodalibus,
jam te nil miseret, dure, tui dulcis amiculi?

jam me prodere, jam non dubitas fallere, perfide?
num facta impia fallacum hominum caelicolis placent?

cum tu neglegis ac me miserum deseris in malis,   5
eheu, quid faciant, dic, homines, cuive habeant fidem?

certe tute jubebas animam tradere, inique, me
inducens in amorem, quasi tuta omnia mi forent.

idem nunc retrahis te ac tua dicta omnia factaque
ventos irrita ferre ac nebulas aerias sinis.   10

si tu oblitus es, at di meminerunt, meminit Fides,
quae te ut paeniteat postmodo facti faciet tui.

XXXI

Paene insularum, Sirmio, insularumque
ocelle, quascumque in liquentibus stagnis
marique vasto fert uterque Neptunus,
quam te libenter quamque laetus inviso,
vix mi ipse credens Thyniam atque Bithynos   5
liquisse campos et videre te in tuto!
o quid solutis est beatius curis,
cum mens onus reponit, ac peregrino
labore fessi venimus larem ad nostrum
desideratoque acquiescimus lecto?   10
hoc est quod unumst pro laboribus tantis.
salve, venusta Sirmio, atque ero gaude
gaudente; vosque, limpidae lacus undae,
ridete quidquid est domi cachinnorum!

Betrayal by a friend

Alfenus, treacherous and false to loyal comrades,
do you now not pity, cruel one, your cherished friend?

Do you now not hesitate to deceive and betray me, traitor?
Think you that the sins of betrayers please the gods above?

When you ignore me and abandon me in my sorry plight,
ah, tell me, what is the world to do, whom is it to trust?

Surely, villain, you kept asking me to give you my soul,
leading me on to love you as though I had nothing to fear?

Yet now you pull back and let the winds and airy clouds
sweep all your words and deeds away to nothingness.

Though you forget, the gods remember, Honour remembers too:
she will one day make you repent of what you have done.

Home, sweet home

Sirmio, gem of all-but-islands and of islands
one and all that on fresh water
or vast ocean either sea-god bears,
how glad, how happy I am to set eyes on you,
hardly believing that Thynia and Bithynian plains are left
behind and I look upon you safe and sound!
What joy is sweeter than the riddance of one's cares,
when the mind lays down its burden, and wearied with the
toil of distant travel we come to our own hearth
and rest upon the bed for which we longed?
This single pleasure makes amends for all our toil.
Hail, lovely Sirmio! Rejoice in your master's joy!
And you, ye crystal waters of the lake,
ripple out all the merriment you have at home!

XXXII

Amabo, mea dulcis Ipsitilla,
meae deliciae, mei lepores,
jube ad te veniam meridiatum.
et si jusseris, illud adjuvato,
nequis liminis obseret tabellam,   5
neu tibi libeat foras abire,
sed domi maneas paresque nobis
novem continuas fututiones.
verum, siquid ages, statim jubeto:
nam pransus jaceo et satur supinus   10
pertundo tunicamque palliumque.

XXXIII

O furum optime balneariorum
Vibenni pater et cinaede fili
(nam dextra pater inquinatiore,
culo filius est voraciore),
cur non exilium malasque in oras   5
itis, quandoquidem patris rapinae
notae sunt populo, et nates pilosas,
fili, non potes asse venditare?

L'Après-midi d'un faune

Please, my darling Ipsitilla,
my beloved, my delight,
invite me to your place to spend the afternoon.
And if you do, have the further kindness to see
that no one locks the panel on your threshold,
and don't take it into your head to go out,
but stay at home and have ready for me
nine consecutive copulations.
And invite me at once if you are going to at all:
for I'm on my bed after lunch, supine and fed,
thrusting through tunic and cloak.

A depraved pair

Prince of thieves at the baths,
father Vibennius, and you, his pansy son
(for father has a more corrupt hand,
the son a greedier arse),
be off the pair of you to exile on accursed
shores, since father's thefts
are common knowledge and as for you, son,
you can't sell your hairy buttocks for a penny!

XXXIV

Dianae sumus in fide
puellae et pueri integri:
Dianam pueri integri
    puellaeque canamus.

o Latonia, maximi   5
magna progenies Jovis,
quam mater prope Deliam
    deposivit olivam,

montium domina ut fores
silvarumque virentium   10
saltuumque reconditorum
    amniumque sonantum:

tu Lucina dolentibus
Juno dicta puerperis,
tu potens Trivia et notho's   15
    dicta lumine Luna.

tu cursu, dea, menstruo
metiens iter annuum,
rustica agricolae bonis
    tecta frugibus exples.   20

sis quocumque tibi placet
sancta nomine, Romulique,
antique ut solita's, bona
    sospites ope gentem.

Hymn to Diana

ALL

Under Diana's care are we,
girls and boys unmarried.
Of Diana let us sing,
    unmarried boys and girls.

GIRLS

Child of Latona, mighty
offspring of mightiest Jove,
whom your mother brought forth
    by the Delian olive

BOYS

to be mistress of the hills
and leafy woods
and sequestered glens
    and splashing streams:

GIRLS

you are invoked as Juno Lucina
by women in the pangs of childbirth,
you, as the magic Lady of the Crossways
    and as Moon of borrowed light.

BOYS

You, goddess, with monthly course
measuring the journey of the year,
fill full with goodly harvest
    the farmer's rustic home.

ALL

Be hallowed under whatever name
it please you; and, as you were wont
in days of yore, succour with goodly aid
    the race of Romulus.

XXXV

Poetae tenero, meo sodali,
velim Caecilio, papyre, dicas
Veronam veniat, Novi relinquens
Comi moenia Lariumque litus:
nam quasdam volo cogitationes   5
amici accipiat sui tuique.

quare, si sapiet, viam vorabit,
quamvis candida milies puella
euntem revocet, manusque collo
ambas iniciens roget morari,   10
quae nunc, si mihi vera nuntiantur,
illum deperit impotente amore.

nam quo tempore legit incohatam
Dindymi dominam, ex eo misellae
ignes interiorem edunt medullam.   15
ignosco tibi, Sapphica puella
musa doctior: est enim venuste
Magna Caecilio incohata Mater.

Invitation to Caecilius

Papyrus page, I should like you to tell
my friend Caecilius, the love-poet,
to come to Verona, leaving the walls
of Novum Comum and Lake Larius' shore:
for I want him to hear some thoughts
of a friend of his and yours.

So, if he's wise, he'll gobble up the journey,
though a pretty girl a thousand times
should call him back from going and, casting both
arms about his neck, should entreat him to delay,
the very girl who now, if reports I hear are true,
loves him to distraction with an uncontrollable love.

For ever since she read the beginning
of his 'Lady of Dindymus,' fires have been
eating away the poor girl's inmost marrow.
I pardon you, maiden more poetical
than the Sapphic Muse: for Caecilius has made
a lovely beginning to his 'Great Mother.'

XXXVI

Annales Volusi, cacata charta,
votum solvite pro mea puella:
nam sanctae Veneri Cupidinique
vovit, si sibi restitutus essem
desissemque truces vibrare iambos,   5
electissima pessimi poetae
scripta tardipedi deo daturam
infelicibus ustulanda lignis.
et hoc pessima se puella vidit
jocose ac lepide vovere divis.   10

nunc, o caeruleo creata ponto,
quae sanctum Idalium Uriosque apertos,
quaeque Ancona Cnidumque harundinosam
colis, quaeque Amathunta, quaeque Golgos,
quaeque Dyrrachium, Hadriae tabernam,   15
acceptum face redditumque votum,
si non illepidum neque invenustumst.
at vos interea venite in ignem,
pleni ruris et inficetiarum
annales Volusi, cacata charta!   20

A vow of Lesbia's

Annals of Volusius, you shitty sheets,
discharge a vow in my sweetheart's name:
for she vowed to holy Venus and Cupid
that, if I were restored to her
and ceased to launch vicious lampoons,
she would give the choicest writings
of the worst of poets to the limping deity
to burn with wood from a barren tree.
And the naughty girl realised that this vow
to the gods was a pretty piece of fun.

Now therefore, daughter of the azure deep,
who dwell in holy Idalium and Urii wide of prospect,
who dwell in Ancon and reedy Cnidus
and in Amathus and in Golgi
and in Dyrrachium, tavern of the Adriatic,
enter the vow as received and duly paid,
as surely as it is not without wit and charm.
But you, meanwhile, come into the fire,
brimful of country clumsiness,
Annals of Volusius, you shitty sheets.

XXXVII

Salax taberna vosque contubernales,
a pilleatis nona fratribus pila,
solis putatis esse mentulas vobis,
solis licere, quidquid est puellarum,
confutvere et putare ceteros hircos?   5
an, continenter quod sedetis insulsi
centum an ducenti, non putatis ausurum
me una ducentos irrumare sessores?
atqui putate: namque totius vobis
frontem tabernae sopionibus scribam.   10

puella nam mi, quae meo sinu fugit,
amata tantum quantum amabitur nulla,
pro qua mihi sunt magna bella pugnata,
consedit istic. hanc boni beatique
omnes amatis, et quidem, quod indignumst,   15
omnes pusilli et semitarii moechi;
tu praeter omnes une de capillatis,
cuniculosae Celtiberiae fili,
Egnati, opaca quem bonum facit barba
et dens Hibera defricatus urina.   20

A house of ill-fame

You regulars of the whore-house tavern
nine doors along from the Capped Brothers,
do you think that you alone have cocks,
that you alone may screw all the girls,
and that the rest of us stink like goats?
Or because you creeps sit in a line, a hundred
or two hundred strong, do you think I wouldn't dare
to stuff the lot of you together as you sit?
Think so if you like: for I'm going to scribble
obscenities against you all over the tavern front.

For the girl who fled my embrace,
she I loved as no woman will ever be loved again,
for whom mighty wars were waged by me, has set up
her pitch there. All you men of rank and fortune
are her lovers, and indeed, to her shame,
all the petty lechers of the backstreets,
you above all, you prince of the long-haired,
Egnatius, you son of rabbit-ridden
Celtiberia, given class by your bushy beard
and teeth that are brushed with Spanish piss.

XXXVIII

Malest, Cornifici, tuo Catullo,
malest, me hercule, et est laboriose,
et magis magis in dies et horas.
quem tu, quod minimum facillimumquest,
qua solatus es allocutione?   5
irascor tibi. sic tuos amores?
paulum quidlibet allocutionis,
maestius lacrimis Simonideis!

XXXIX

Egnatius, quod candidos habet dentes,
renidet usque quaque. si ad rei ventumst
subsellium, cum orator excitat fletum,
renidet ille. si ad pii rogum fili
lugetur, orba cum flet unicum mater,   5
renidet ille. quidquid est, ubicumquest,
quodcumque agit, renidet. hunc habet morbum,
neque elegantem, ut arbitror, neque urbanum.
quare monendumst te mihi, bone Egnati.
si urbanus esses aut Sabinus aut Tiburs   10
aut pinguis Umber aut obesus Etruscus
aut Lanuvinus ater atque dentatus
aut Transpadanus, ut meos quoque attingam,
aut quilibet, qui puriter lavit dentes,
tamen renidere usque quaque te nollem: 15
nam risu inepto res ineptior nullast.
nunc Celtiber es: Celtiberia in terra,
quod quisque minxit, hoc sibi solet mane
dentem atque russam defricare gingivam,
ut, quo iste vester expolitior dens est,   20
hoc te amplius bibisse praedicet loti.

Catullus unwell

Your Catullus feels unwell, Cornificius,
he feels unwell, dammit, frightfully unwell,
and getting worse every day and hour.
And what word of comfort have you had for him,
the slightest and easiest thing to give? I'm wild
with you. Is this how you treat your pal?
Just send some little word of comfort,
sadder than Simonidean tears.

Spanish dentifrice

Because Egnatius has white teeth,
he smiles wherever he goes. If he's come to support the
prisoner at the bar, when the advocate is drawing tears,
he smiles; if there is mourning at the pyre of a dear son,
when the bereaved mother is weeping for her only child,
he smiles. Whatever the occasion, wherever he is,
whatever he does, he smiles. It is a disease he has,
not an elegant one, I think, or in good taste.
So I must have a word with you, my good Egnatius.
If you were a man from Rome or a Sabine or a Tiburtine
or a plump Umbrian or a fat Etruscan
or a dark and toothy Lanuvian
or a Transpadane, to touch on my own people too,
or anyone else who washes his teeth with clean water,
I still shouldn't want you to smile wherever you go:
for there's nothing more foolish than a foolish grin.
As it is, you are a Spaniard: now in the land of Spain
everyone regularly brushes his teeth and ruddy gums
in the morning with his piddle,
so that, the more highly polished your teeth are,
the more urine they will prove you to have swallowed.

XL

Quaenam te mala mens, miselle Raude,
agit praecipitem in meos iambos?
quis deus tibi non bene advocatus
vecordem parat excitare rixam?
an ut pervenias in ora vulgi?   5
quid vis? qualibet esse notus optas?
eris, quandoquidem meos amores
cum longa voluisti amare poena.

XLI

Anneiana puella defututa
tota milia me decem poposcit,
ista turpiculo puella naso,
decoctoris amica Formiani.
propinqui, quibus est puella curae,   5
amicos medicosque convocate:
non est sana puella, nec rogare,
qualis sit, solet aes imaginosum.

Insensate craving for fame

What infatuation, lovesick Ravidus,
drives you headlong into my lampoons?
What god invoked by you in an evil hour
makes haste to start the frantic duel?
Is it because you want to be on people's lips?
What are you after? Do you desire to be known,
no matter how? So you shall be, since you've chosen
to love my loved one and be pilloried for ever.

The girl from Anneianum

A well-laid girl from Anneianum
has had the nerve to ask me for a cool ten grand,
I mean the girl with the ugly snub nose,
the mistress of the Formian bankrupt.
You relatives who have charge of the girl
had better call her friends and doctors in:
the girl's not right in the head, and has no thought
of asking the mirror what she looks like.

XLII

Adeste, hendecasyllabi, quot estis
omnes, undique, quotquot estis omnes.
jocum me putat esse moecha turpis,
et negat mihi nostra reddituram
pugillaria, si pati potestis.   5
persequamur eam et reflagitemus.

quae sit, quaeritis? illa, quam videtis
turpe incedere, mimice ac moleste
ridentem catuli ore Gallicani.
circumsistite eam, et reflagitate: 10
'moecha putida, redde codicillos,
redde, putida moecha, codicillos!'

non assis facit? o lutum, lupanar,
aut si perditius potest quid esse!
sed non est tamen hoc satis putandum.   15
conclamate iterum altiore voce: 18
'moecha putida, redde codicillos,
redde, putida moecha, codicillos!'   20

sed nil proficimus, nihil movetur.
mutandast ratio modusque vobis,
siquid proficere amplius potestis,   23
quo, si non aliud potest, ruborem   16
ferreo canis exprimamus ore: 17
'pudica et proba, redde codicillos!'   24

Demand for restitution

Come hither, hendecasyllables, all of you there are,
from every quarter, all of you there are.
An impudent harlot takes me for a fool
and says, if you please,
she'll not return my writing-tablets.
Let's go after her and demand them back.

You ask who she is? Why, she's the one you see
strutting impudently and, in vulgar and annoying fashion,
laughing with her mouth agape like a Gallic hound.
Crowd round her and accost her with your demands:
'Filthy harlot, return the tablets,
return the tablets, filthy harlot!'

She takes no notice? Oh the tart, the trollop,
and whatever's worse than that!
But even so we mustn't let it go at this.
Call out once more in a louder voice:
'Filthy harlot, return the tablets,
return the tablets, filthy harlot!'

We've got nowhere, she isn't moved at all.
You must change your plan and tactics
if you are to make any headway, so that, if
nothing else is possible, we may at least force
a blush from the face of the brassy bitch:
'Return the tablets, chaste and honourable lady!'

XLIII

Salve, nec minimo puella naso
nec bello pede nec nigris ocellis
nec longis digitis nec ore sicco
nec sane nimis elegante lingua,
decoctoris amica Formiani.   5
ten provincia narrat esse bellam?
tecum Lesbia nostra comparatur?
o saeclum insipiens et inficetum!

XLIV

O funde noster seu Sabine seu Tiburs—
nam te esse Tiburtem autumant, quibus non est
cordi Catullum laedere; at quibus cordist,
quovis Sabinum pignore esse contendunt—
sed seu Sabine sive verius Tiburs,   5
fui libenter in tua suburbana
villa malamque pectore expuli tussim,
non immerenti quam mihi meus venter,
dum sumptuosas appeto, dedit, cenas.
nam, Sestianus dum volo esse conviva,   10
orationem in Antium petitorem
plenam veneni et pestilentiae legi.
hic me gravedo frigida et frequens tussis
quassavit usque dum in tuum sinum fugi
et me recuravi otioque et urtica.   15
quare refectus maximas tibi grates
ago, meum quod non es ulta peccatum.
nec deprecor jam, si nefaria scripta
Sesti recepso, quin gravedinem et tussim
non mi, sed ipsi Sestio ferat frigus,   20
qui tunc vocat me, cum malum librum fecit.

No rival for Lesbia

Greetings, lady, who have neither dainty nose,
nor pretty feet, nor dark eyes,
nor slender fingers, nor dry lips,
and certainly not a very refined tongue,
you who are the mistress of the Formian bankrupt.
Are you the lady the province calls beautiful?
Are you the one my Lesbia is compared to?
What a senseless, tasteless age we live in!

A speech of Sestius's

O farm of mine, be you Sabine or Tiburtine—
for those who have no wish to offend Catullus
assert that you are Tiburtine, whilst whose who have
lay any odds that you are Sabine—
but be you Sabine or (more rightly) Tiburtine,
I enjoyed my stay in your retreat between town and
country, and from my chest shook off a nasty cough,
which—serve me right!—my stomach gave me
while I was hankering after sumptuous dinners.
For, wanting to dine with Sestius,
I read a speech of his against Antius's candidacy
full of poisonous and pestilent stuff.
Hereupon a shivering cold and hacking cough
gave me convulsions until I fled to your bosom
and nursed myself well with a diet of rest and a tisane.
So, now restored to health, I send you warmest
thanks because you did not punish my error.
Nor do I now object, if ever again I take up Sestius's
vile writings, to their frigidity bringing a cold and
a cough, not upon me, but upon Sestius himself,
who only invites me when he has produced a nasty book.

XLV

Acmen Septimius, suos amores,
tenens in gremio 'mea' inquit 'Acme,
ni te perdite amo atque amare porro
omnes sum assidue paratus annos,
quantum qui pote plurimum perire,   5
solus in Libya Indiaque tosta
caesio veniam obvius leoni.'
hoc ut dixit, Amor, sinistra ut ante,
dextra sternuit approbationem.

at Acme leviter caput reflectens   10
et dulcis pueri ebrios ocellos
illo purpureo ore saviata,
'sic,' inquit 'mea vita, Septimille,
huic uni domino usque serviamus,
ut multo mihi major acriorque   15
ignis mollibus ardet in medullis.'
hoc ut dixit, Amor, sinistra ut ante,
dextra sternuit approbationem.

nunc ab auspicio bono profecti
mutuis animis amant amantur: 20
unam Septimius misellus Acmen
mavult quam Syrias Britanniasque;
uno in Septimio fidelis Acme
facit delicias libidinesque.
quis ullos homines beatiores   25
vidit, quis Venerem auspicatiorem?

Love duet

Septimius, holding his darling Acme
in his arms, said, 'Acme mine,
unless I love you to desperation and am ready
to go on loving you constantly for all time to come,
as desperately as the most desperate of lovers,
may I on my own in Libya or parched India
come face to face with a green-eyed lion.'
As he said this, Love first on the left
and then on the right sneezed approval.

But Acme, gently bending back her head
and kissing the dear boy's drunken eyes
with those rosy lips of hers,
said, 'Dear Septimius, all my life's desire,
so may we ever serve this master alone,
as surely as a much greater and fiercer
flame burns in my soft marrow.'
As she said this, Love first on the left
and then on the right sneezed approval.

Now setting out from this happy omen
they love and are loved with mutual affection:
love-lorn Septimius prefers Acme alone
to any Syria or Britain;
in Septimius alone does faithful Acme
take all her pleasure and delight.
Who ever saw more blessed mortals,
who a more auspicious love?

XLVI

Jam ver egelidos refert tepores,
jam caeli furor aequinoctialis
jucundis Zephyri silescit auris.
linquantur Phrygii, Catulle, campi
Nicaeaeque ager uber aestuosae: 5
ad claras Asiae volemus urbes.
jam mens praetrepidans avet vagari,
jam laeti studio pedes vigescunt.
o dulces comitum valete coetus,
longe quos simul a domo profectos   10
diversae varie viae reportant!

XLVII

Porci et Socration, duae sinistrae
Pisonis, scabies famesque munda,
vos Veraniolo meo et Fabullo
verpus praeposuit Priapus ille?
vos convivia lauta sumptuose   5
de die facitis, mei sodales
quaerunt in trivio vocationes?

XLVIII

Mellitos oculos tuos, Juventi,
siquis me sinat usque basiare,
usque ad milia basiem trecenta,
nec mi umquam videar satur futurus,
non si densior Africis aristis   5
sit nostrae seges osculationis.

Goodbye to all that!

Now spring brings back the warmth that banishes the frosts,
now the fury of the equinoctial sky
is hushed before the zephyr's genial breezes.
Be off, Catullus, from the plains of Phrygia
and sultry Nicaea's fertile fields!
Let me take flight to the famed cities of Asia.
Now in a flutter of anticipation my heart longs to roam,
now my feet quicken with happy eagerness.
Farewell, dear band of comrades,
who left home together upon our distant journey
and separately by different routes are again brought back!

Piso's favourites

Porcius and Socration, you two thieving tools
of Piso, bringers of sheer plague and famine,
are you preferred to my dear Veranius and
Fabullus by that horny Priapus?
Are you at vast expense holding splendid banquets
before the day's work is done, while friends of mine
are angling for invitations at street-corners?

Kissing Juventius

If anyone let me go on kissing
your honey-sweet eyes, Juventius,
I should kiss them up to three-hundred thousand times
nor ever think I had had enough,
not even if the harvest of our kissing
were thicker than Africa's ears of corn.

XLIX

Disertissime Romuli nepotum,
quot sunt quotque fuere, Marce Tulli,
quotque post aliis erunt in annis,
gratias tibi maximas Catullus
agit pessimus omnium poeta,   5
tanto pessimus omnium poeta,
quanto tu optimus omnium patronus.

L

Hesterno, Licini, die otiosi
multum lusimus in tuis tabellis,
ut convenerat esse delicatos:
scribens versiculos uterque nostrum
ludebat numero modo hoc modo illoc,   5
reddens mutua per jocum atque vinum.
atque illinc abii tuo lepore
incensus, Licini, facetiisque,
ut nec me miserum cibus juvaret,
nec somnus tegeret quiete ocellos,   10
sed toto, indomitus furore, lecto
versarer cupiens videre lucem,
ut tecum loquerer, simulque ut essem.
at defessa labore membra postquam
semimortua lectulo jacebant,   15
hoc, jucunde, tibi poema feci,
ex quo perspiceres meum dolorem.
nunc audax cave sis, precesque nostras,
oramus, cave despuas, ocelle,
ne poenas Nemesis reposcat a te.   20
est vemens dea: laedere hanc caveto.

Thank you, Cicero

Most eloquent of the descendants of Romulus
that are or have been, Marcus Tullius,
or will yet be in years to come,
you are sent hearty thanks by Catullus,
him who is the worst poet of all,
as much indeed the worst poet of all
as you are the best advocate of all.

Neoterics at play

Yesterday, Licinius, with nothing to do
we had much sport on your tablets,
having agreed to enjoy ourselves:
each of us writing pretty verses
took his pleasure now in this metre, now in that,
exchanging sallies amid jesting and drinking.
And then I came away from this so excited
by your wit and pleasantry, Licinius,
that neither could food satisfy my poor body
nor sleep veil my eyes in peace,
but with uncontrollable delirium I tossed
all over the bed, longing to see the dawn,
that with you I might talk, that with you I might be.
But when my limbs were worn out with fatigue
and lay half-dead upon the bed,
I composed this poem for you, my dear friend,
that from it you might learn my suffering:
Now beware of being haughty and of scorning
my entreaty, I beg you, bosom pal,
lest Nemesis claim a penalty from you.
She's an impetuous goddess: beware of offending her.

LI

Ille mi par esse deo videtur,
ille, si fas est, superare divos,
qui sedens adversus identidem te
    spectat et audit

dulce ridentem, misero quod omnes   5
eripit sensus mihi : nam simul te,
Lesbia, aspexi, nihil est super mi
    vocis in ore ;

lingua sed torpet, tenuis sub artus
flamma demanat, sonitu suopte   10
tintinant aures geminae, teguntur
    lumina nocte.

otium, Catulle, tibi molestumst :
otio exsultas nimiumque gestis :
otium et reges prius et beatas   15
    perdidit urbes.

To Clodia, who henceforth becomes Lesbia

He seems to me the equal of a god,
he seems, if that may be, the gods' superior,
who sits face to face with you and again and again
    watches and hears you

sweetly laughing, an experience which robs me
poor wretch, of all my senses; for the moment I set
eyes on you, Lesbia, there remains not a whisper
    of voice on my lips,

but my tongue is paralysed, a subtle flame
courses through my limbs, with sound self-caused
my two ears ring, and my eyes are
    covered in darkness.

Idleness, Catullus, is your trouble;
idleness is what delights you and moves you to passion;
idleness has proved ere now the ruin of kings and
    prosperous cities.

LII

Quid est, Catulle? quid moraris emori?
sella in curuli struma Nonius sedet,
per consulatum pejerat Vatinius:
quid est, Catulle? quid moraris emori?

LIII

Risi nescioquem modo e corona,
qui, cum mirifice Vatiniana
meus crimina Calvus explicasset,
admirans ait haec manusque tollens,
'di magni, salaputium disertum!'   5

LIV

Othonis caput oppido pusillum
et, trirustice, semilauta crura,
subtile et leve peditum Libonis,
si non omnia, displicere vellem
tibi et Fufidio, seni recocto: 5
irascere iterum meis iambis
immerentibus, unice imperator.

Vatinius's consulship

What stops you, Catullus? Why wait to die and end it all?
There's Nonius the wart sitting in a curule chair,
and Vatinius falsely swearing by his consulship.
What stops you, Catullus? Why wait to die and end it all?

A witty remark

I had a laugh just now at someone in the court,
who, when my friend Calvus had splendidly
unfolded the wickedness of Vatinius,
threw up his hands and cried in admiration
'Great gods, what an eloquent little cock!'

The general without peer

I could wish, you utter bumpkin, that Otho's
downright puny head and half-washed legs
and Libo's smooth and subtle farting,
if not everything else about them, should revolt
you and that warmed up greybeard Fufidius:
once more will you be enraged by my
innocent lampoons, O general without peer!

LV

Oramus, si forte non molestumst,
   demonstres ubi sint tuae latebrae.
te in campo quaesivimus minore,
   te in circo, te in omnibus sacellis,
te in templo summi Jovis sacrato.   5
   in Magni simul ambulatione
femellas omnes, amice, prendi;
   quas vultu video tamen serenas.
'aufertis' sic usque flagitabam
   'Camerjum mihi, pessimae puellae?'   10
'en,' inquit quaedam, sinum reducens,
   'en hic in roseis latet papillis!'

sed te jam ferre Herculi labos est:
   nec te prendere nunc, amice, possim,
non custos si fingar ille Cretum,   (LVIII 6)
   non Ladas ego pinnipesve Perseus,   (8)
   non si Pegaseo ferar volatu,   (7)
   non Rhesi niveae citaeque bigae;
   adde huc plumipedas volatilesque,   (10)
   ventorumque simul require cursum,
   quos junctos, Cameri, mihi dicares:
defessus tamen omnibus medullis
et multis languoribus peresus
   essem te mihi, amice, quaeritando.   (15)

tanto te in fastu negas, amice?   14
   dic nobis ubi sis futurus, ede
audacter, committe, crede luci.
   num te lacteolae tenent puellae?
si linguam clauso tenes in ore,
   fructus proicies amoris omnes:
verbosa gaudet Venus loquella.   20
   vel, si vis, licet obseres palatum,
dum nostri sis particeps amoris.

Come out, wherever you are!
I beg you, if it isn't any trouble,
    show me where your hide-out is.
I've searched for you everywhere, from the little Campus
    to the Circus, from every little shrine
to the sacred temple of Jupiter Most High.
    Then, my friend, in Pompey's colonnade
I waylaid the street-walkers,
    though I see them all wearing innocent expressions.
'Are you hiding Camerius from me, you
    naughty girls?' I kept asking them.
'Here,' said one, opening up her dress,
    'here he is, concealed between my rosy breasts!'

But to put up with you now is a labour of Hercules:
        nor could I catch you now, my friend,
even were I to be made into the fabled sentinel of Crete,
    or Ladas or wing-sandalled Perseus,
    or were to soar on high with the flight of Pegasus
    or of Rhesus's swift and snowy pair of steeds;
    add to these the feather-footed and flying creatures
    and summon thereto the speed of the winds,
    all which, Camerius, though you should give me harnessed:
    I should still be wearied in every limb
and utterly exhausted from frequent fainting,
    my friend, in searching for you.

Why do you withhold yourself so haughtily, my friend?
    Tell me where you're going to be, out with it
boldly, trust me with it, bring it out into the open.
    Will some tender little girls not let you go?
If you shut your mouth and hold your tongue,
    you'll let go all the fruits of love:
Venus rejoices in loquacious speech.
    Or, if you like, you may seal your lips,
so long as you don't run away from my love.

LVI

O rem ridiculam, Cato, et jocosam,
dignamque auribus et tuo cachinno!
ride, quidquid amas, Cato, Catullum:
res est ridicula et nimis jocosa.
deprendi modo pupulum puellae   5
trusantem: hunc ego, si placet Dionae,
protelo rigida mea cecidi.

LVII

Pulchre convenit improbis cinaedis,
Mamurrae pathicoque Caesarique.
nec mirum: maculae pares utrisque,
urbana altera et illa Formiana,
impressae resident nec eluentur: 5
morbosi pariter, gemelli utrique,
uno in lecticulo erudituli ambo,
non hic quam ille magis vorax adulter,
rivales socii puellularum.
pulchre convenit improbis cinaedis.   10

A comic situation

O what an absurd and funny story, Cato,
good enough for you to hear and snigger at!
So laugh, Cato, if you've any love for Catullus:
it really is an absurd and funny story.
I just now caught sweetheart's pet
wanking, and (so help me the mother of Venus)
I beat him with my hard cane—in tandem!

Arcades ambo

Those shameless buggers are finely matched,
pansy Mamurra and Caesar.
And no wonder: similar stains,
one a city dye, the other a dye of Formiae,
are stamped upon the pair and never will be washed away.
Tainted alike they are, a pair of identical twins,
two dilettante pedants on a single study-couch,
one as greedy an adulterer as the other,
rival partners in their pursuit of girls.
Yes, those shameless buggers are finely matched.

LVIII

Caeli, Lesbia nostra, Lesbia illa,
illa Lesbia, quam Catullus unam
plus quam se atque suos amavit omnes,
nunc in quadriviis et angiportis
glubit magnanimos Remi nepotes.   5

LIX

Bononiensis Rufa Rufulum fellat,
uxor Meneni, saepe quam in sepulcretis
vidistis ipso rapere de rogo cenam,
cum devolutum ex igne prosequens panem
ab semiraso tunderetur ustore.   5

LX

Num te leaena montibus Libystinis
aut Scylla latrans infima inguinum parte
tam mente dura procreavit ac taetra,
ut supplicis vocem in novissimo casu
contemptam haberes, ah nimis fero corde?   5

Lesbia's degradation

Caelius, our Lesbia, the peerless Lesbia,
the Lesbia that Catullus once loved above all, more than
himself and all his nearest and dearest put together,
now haunts the street-corners and alleys,
sapping the great-souled descendants of Remus.

Pasquinade

Rufa of Bononia puts her lips to her Rufus,
Rufa, Menenius' wife, whom ye have often seen in the
graveyard snatching a meal from the funeral pyre
and whilst reaching for a loaf fallen from the fire
getting buggered by a half-shaven corpse-burner.

Inhumanity

Was it some lioness on Afric hills
or a Scylla barking from her womb below
that bore you to have a mind so hard and inhuman
as to treat with scorn a suppliant's plea
in his last need, ah, too cruel-hearted one?

LXI

Collis o Heliconii
cultor, Uraniae genus,
qui rapis teneram ad virum
virginem, o Hymenaee Hymen,
   o Hymen Hymenaee,   5

cinge tempora floribus
suave olentis amaraci,
flammeum cape, laetus huc,
huc veni, niveo gerens
   luteum pede soccum;   10

excitusque hilari die,
nuptialia concinens
voce carmina tinnula,
pelle humum pedibus, manu
   pineam quate taedam.   15

namque Junia Manlio,
qualis Idalium colens
venit ad Phrygium Venus
judicem, bona cum bona
   nubet alite virgo,   20

floridis velut enitens
myrtus Asia ramulis,
quos Hamadryades deae
ludicrum sibi roscido
   nutriuntur honore.   25

Nuptial song for Junia and Manlius

INVOCATION TO HYMEN
You who dwell on Helicon's
mount, son of Urania,
you who bear off a tender bride
to her groom, O Hymeneal Hymen,
    O Hymen Hymeneal,

bind your brows with blossoms
of fragrant marjoram,
take the bridal veil, and joyfully hither,
hither come, wearing on your snow-white
    feet the yellow sandal,

and stirred by this happy day
swell with your silvery voice
our wedding songs, beat the ground
with dancing feet, and in your hand
    shake the pine torch.

For fair as Venus,
Idalium's queen, when she appeared
before the Phrygian judge,
Junia is to wed Manlius,
    fair maiden with fair omen,

like the Asian myrtle
shining with flowery sprays
which the wood-nymphs
nurture with meed of dew
    as playthings for themselves.

quare age, huc aditum ferens,
perge linquere Thespiae
rupis Aonios specus,
nympha quos super irrigat
    frigerans Aganippe,   30

ac domum dominam voca
conjugis cupidam novi,
mentem amore revinciens,
ut tenax hedera huc et huc
    arborem implicat errans.   35

vosque item simul, integrae
virgines, quibus advenit
par dies, agite in modum
dicite, 'o Hymenaee Hymen,
    o Hymen Hymenaee,'   40

ut libentius, audiens
se citarier ad suum
munus, huc aditum ferat
dux bonae Veneris, boni
    conjugator amoris.   45

quis deus magis anxiis
est petendus amantibus?
quem colent homines magis
caelitum, o Hymenaee Hymen,
    o Hymen Hymenaee?   50

te suis tremulus parens
invocat, tibi virgines
zonula soluunt sinus,
te timens cupida novus
    captat aure maritus.   55

Come then, make your way hither,
and hasten to leave the Aonian
grottoes of the Thespian rock,
which the nymph Aganippe sprinkles
    with cold water from above,

and call home home's mistress
with yearning for her bridegroom,
binding her heart with love's meshes,
as the clinging ivy roaming here and there
    entwines the tree.

And you too, unwed maidens,
for whom a like day is at hand,
come, sing in unison with me
'O Hymeneal Hymen,
    O Hymen Hymeneal,'

that all the more readily, hearing
himself summoned to his rightful office,
the god may make his approach hither,
forerunner of honest passion,
    uniter of honest love.

Which god is more fit to be
invoked by heart-sick lovers?
Which of the gods shall mortals
worship more, O Hymeneal Hymen,
    O Hymen Hymeneal?

You the aged father invokes
for his children, for you the girls
untie the girdle of their robes,
for you the anxious bridegroom
    listens with eager ear.

tu fero juveni in manus
floridam ipse puellulam
dedis a gremio suae
matris, o Hymenaee Hymen,
   o Hymen Hymenaee.   60

nil potest sine te Venus,
fama quod bona comprobet,
commodi capere: at potest
te volente. quis huic deo
   compararier ausit?   65

nulla quit sine te domus
liberos dare, nec parens
stirpe nitier: at potest
te volente. quis huic deo
   compararier ausit?   70

quae tuis careat sacris,
non queat dare praesides
terra finibus: at queat
te volente. quis huic deo
   compararier ausit?   75

claustra pandite januae!
virgo, ades! viden ut faces
splendidas quatiunt comas?
cur moraris? abit dies:
   prodeas, nova nupta.

neve respicias domum,
quae fuit tua, neu pedes
tardet ingenuus pudor.
quem tamen magis audiens   80
   fles, quod ire necessest.

You yourself put into the hands of an
ardent youth the blossoming maid
you have snatched from her mother's
bosom, O Hymeneal Hymen,
    O Hymen Hymeneal!

Without you Venus can take no pleasure
that honorable report may approve:
but with your consent
she can. With such a god
    who dares compare?

Without you no house can
provide children, no one become a father
supported by an heir: but with your consent
he can. With such a god
    who dares compare?

Without your rites no land can
provide guards to defend
its boundaries: but with your consent
it can. With such a god
    who dares compare?

SUMMONS TO THE BRIDE

Open ye the fastenings of the door!
Come hither, bride! Do you see how the torches
shake their resplendent tresses?
Why do you tarry? Day slips by:
    come forth, O bride.

And look not back on the home
that was yours, nor let your feet
be delayed by noble modesty.
But heeding this all the more, you weep,
    because it is necessary to go.

flere desine: non tibi, Au-
runculeia, periculumst,
nequa femina pulchrior
clarum ab Oceano diem   85
   viderit venientem.

talis in vario solet
divitis domini hortulo
stare flos hyacinthinus.
sed moraris, abit dies: 90
   prodeas, nova nupta.

prodeas, nova nupta, si
jam videtur, et audias
nostra verba. viden? faces
aureas quatiunt comas: 95
   prodeas, nova nupta.

non tuus levis in mala
deditus vir adultera,
probra turpia persequens,
a tuis teneris volet   100
   secubare papillis,

lenta sed velut assitas
vitis implicat arbores,
implicabitur in tuum
complexum. sed abit dies: 105
   prodeas, nova nupta.

o cubile, quod omnibus
dignum amoribus instruit
veste purpurea Tyros,
fulcit India eburnei
   candido pede lecti,

Cease weeping: there is no
danger, Aurunculeia,
that any woman more beautiful
has ever seen the bright day
   coming from Ocean.

So in a rich owner's
garden of many colours
stands a hyacinth flower.
But you tarry, day slips by:
   come forth, O bride.

Come forth, O bride, if at last
it please you, and hear
our words. Do you see? The torches
shake their golden tresses:
   come forth, O bride.

Not lightly given to some evil
paramour or following shameful
paths of dishonour
will your husband wish to lie apart
   from your tender bosom,

but, as the pliant vine
entwines the trees planted beside it,
so will he be entwined in your
embrace. But day slips by:
   come forth, O bride.

O bed, which for all
the ways of love has been adorned
by bright coverlets from Tyre
and India supports with an ivory
   couch's shining foot,

quae tuo veniunt ero,
quanta gaudia, quae vaga　　　　　　　110
nocte, quae medio die
gaudeat! sed abit dies:
　　prodeas, nova nupta.

tollite, o pueri, faces:
flammeum video venire.　　　　　　　115
ite concinite in modum
'jo Hymen Hymenaee jo,
　　jo Hymen Hymenaee.'

ne diu taceat procax
Fescennina jocatio,　　　　　　　120
nec nuces pueris neget
desertum domini audiens
　　concubinus amorem.

da nuces pueris, iners
concubine! satis diu　　　　　　　125
lusisti: nucibus juvet
jam servire Talassio.
　　concubine, nuces da.

sordebant tibi vilicae,
concubine, hodie atque heri:　　　　　　　130
nunc tuum cinerarius
tondet os. miser ah miser
　　concubine, nuces da.

diceris male te a tuis
unguentate glabris marite　　　　　　　135
abstinere, sed abstine.
jo Hymen Hymenaee jo,
　　jo Hymen Hymenaee.

what joys lie in store for your master,
for him to enjoy in the vagabond night,
for him at noon of day!
But day slips by:
 come forth, O bride.

BRIDAL PROCESSION

Raise high the torches, boys:
I see the bridal veil approaching.
Come, sing in unison
'O Hymen Hymeneal O,
 O Hymen Hymeneal!'

Let the saucy Fescennine
jesting not long be hushed,
nor let the favourite deny the boys nuts
when he hears that his master's attachment
 has been forsaken.

Scatter the nuts for the boys, idle
favourite! You have sported
long enough: with nuts be it now
your pleasure to serve Talassius.
 Favourite, scatter the nuts!

You turned up your nose at stewards'
wives, favourite, till today:
now the hairdresser shaves
your cheeks. Ah, wretched, wretched
 favourite, scatter the nuts!

They say that you are loth to give up
your hairless pets, perfumed
bridegroom, but give them up.
O Hymen Hymeneal O,
 O Hymen Hymeneal!

scimus haec tibi quae licent
soli cognita, sed marito   140
ista non eadem licent.
jo Hymen Hymenaee jo,
   jo Hymen Hymenaee.

nupta, tu quoque, quae tuus
vir petet, cave ne neges,   145
ni petitum aliunde eat.
jo Hymen Hymenaee jo,
   jo Hymen Hymenaee.

en tibi domus ut potens
et beata viri tui!   150
quae tibi sine serviat—
jo Hymen Hymenaee jo,
   jo Hymen Hymenaee—

usque dum tremulum movens
cana tempus anilitas   155
omnia omnibus adnuit.
jo Hymen Hymenaee jo,
   jo Hymen Hymenaee.

transfer omine cum bono
limen aureolos pedes,   160
rasilemque subi forem.
jo Hymen Hymenaee jo,
   jo Hymen Hymenaee.

aspice, intus ut accubans
vir tuus Tyrio in toro   165
totus immineat tibi.
jo Hymen Hymenaee jo,
   jo Hymen Hymenaee.

We know that the joys permitted
a bachelor are known to you, but
they are not permitted a husband.
O Hymen Hymeneal O,
    O Hymen Hymeneal!

And you too, bride, beware of
refusing what your husband seeks,
in case he go and seek it elsewhere.
O Hymen Hymeneal O,
    O Hymen Hymeneal!

Lo, how powerful and
prosperous is your husband's house!
Deign to receive its service—
O Hymen Hymeneal O,
    O Hymen Hymeneal!—

until hoary old age causes your
head to tremble and nod
assent to all in all things.
O Hymen Hymeneal O,
    O Hymen Hymeneal!

Bear with good omen across
the threshold your golden feet
and pass within the polished door.
O Hymen Hymeneal O,
    O Hymen Hymeneal!

See how your husband, reclining
within on purple couch,
is all intent upon you.
O Hymen Hymeneal O,
    O Hymen Hymeneal!

illi non minus ac tibi
pectore urit in intimo   170
flamma, sed penite magis.
jo Hymen Hymenaee jo,
    jo Hymen Hymenaee.

mitte bracchiolum teres,
praetextate, puellulae: 175
jam cubile adeat viri.
jo Hymen Hymenaee jo,
    jo Hymen Hymenaee.

vos, bonae senibus viris
cognitae bene feminae,   180
collocate puellulam.
jo Hymen Hymenaee jo,
    jo Hymen Hymenaee.

jam licet venias, marite:
uxor in thalamo tibist,   185
ore floridulo nitens,
alba parthenice velut
    luteumve papaver.

at, marite, ita me juvent
caelites, nihilo minus   190
pulcher es, neque te Venus
neglegit. sed abit dies:
    perge, ne remorare.

non diu remoratus es,
jam venis. bona te Venus   195
juverit, quoniam palam
quod cupis cupis, et bonum
    non abscondis amorem.

A flame burns in the depths
of his heart no less than yours,
no less but more profoundly.
O Hymen Hymeneal O,
    O Hymen Hymeneal!

Let go the smooth arm of the maiden,
page with the purple toga:
let her now go to her husband's bed.
O Hymen Hymeneal O,
    O Hymen Hymeneal!

You, worthy matrons worthily wed
to your aged spouses,
set the maiden in her place.
O Hymen Hymeneal O,
    O Hymen Hymeneal!

EPITHALAMIUM

Bridegroom, now you may come:
your wife is in the bridal chamber,
bright with a tender bloom upon her face,
like the white camomile
    or yellow poppy.

Yet, husband, so help me
heaven, you are no less
beautiful, nor does Venus
neglect you. But day slips by:
    hasten, do not tarry.

Not long have you tarried,
you are here already. May kindly Venus
help you, since what you desire,
you desire openly, hiding not
    your honest love.

ille pulveris Africi
siderumque micantium   200
subducat numerum prius,
qui vestri numerare vult
  multa milia ludi.

ludite ut libet, et brevi
liberos date. non decet   205
tam vetus sine liberis
nomen esse, sed indidem
  semper ingenerari.

Torquatus volo parvulus
matris e gremio suae   210
porrigens teneras manus
dulce rideat ad patrem
  semihiante labello.

sit suo similis patri
Manlio, ut facie omnibus   215
noscitetur ab insciis
et pudicitiam suae
  matris indicet ore.

talis illius a bona
matre laus genus approbet,   220
qualis unica ab optima
matre Telemacho manet
  fama Penelopaeo.

claudite ostia, virgines:
lusimus satis. at, boni   225
conjuges, bene vivite et
munere assiduo valentem
  exercete juventam!

Let him who wants to count
the many thousands of your joys
first reckon the number
of the desert sands
 or the twinkling stars.

Sport as you please, and soon
produce children. It is not right
for so old a name to be
without children, but it should ever
 be perpetuated from the same stock.

I long to see a little Torquatus,
holding out baby hands
from his mother's bosom,
smile endearingly at his father
 with tiny lips half-parted.

May he so resemble his father Manlius
that by his features he may be known
to all who are ignorant of his identity
and through his face declare
 his mother's chastity.

May this good name inherited
from a noble mother establish his descent,
like the matchless reputation which devolved
from the noblest of mothers upon Telemachus,
 son of Penelope.

Maidens, close the doors:
enough of our merry song! And you, happy
pair, live happily and
enjoy without stint the functions
 of vigorous youth.

LXII

Vesper adest: juvenes, consurgite: Vesper Olympo
exspectata diu vix tandem lumina tollit.
surgere jam tempus, jam pingues linquere mensas:
jam veniet virgo, jam dicetur hymenaeus.
    Hymen o Hymenaee, Hymen ades o Hymenaee!   5

Cernitis, innuptae, juvenes? consurgite contra:
nimirum Oetaeos ostendit Noctifer ignes.
sic certest: viden ut perniciter exsiluere?
non temere exsiluere: canent quod vincere par est.
    Hymen o Hymenaee, Hymen ades o Hymenaee!   10

Non facilis nobis, aequales, palma paratast:
aspicite, innuptae secum ut meditata requirunt.
non frustra meditantur: habent memorabile quod sit.
nec mirum, penitus quae tota mente laborant.
nos alio mentes, alio divisimus aures;   15
jure igitur vincemur: amat victoria curam.
quare nunc animos saltem convertite vestros:
dicere jam incipient, jam respondere decebit.
    Hymen o Hymenaee, Hymen ades o Hymenaee!

Choral Wedding Song

BOYS

The evening star is here: young men, arise: now at long last
the evening star lifts his much-awaited light into the sky.
Now is it time to rise, now time to leave the rich tables;
now will come the bride, now will the wedding song be sung.
    Hail, Hymen Hymenaeus! Hymen Hymenaeus, come!

GIRLS

Maidens, do you see the boys? Rise up to face them.
Clearly the herald of night shows his fires over Oeta.
Yes, that is it; see how swiftly they leapt up. Not for
nothing leapt they up; theirs will be a song worth beating.
    Hail, Hymen Hymenaeus! Hymen Hymenaeus, come!

BOYS

No easy triumph, comrades, have we ready made.
See how the maidens inwardly recall their studied verses.
Not in vain they study; they have a song worth remembering.
No wonder, since they are striving hard with all their minds.
But we have directed our minds one way and our ears another;
justly then shall we be beaten, for victory loves effort.
Wherefore turn now your minds at least to business;
soon they will start to sing, soon we shall have to reply.
    Hail, Hymen Hymenaeus! Hymen Hymenaeus, come!

Hespere, quis caelo fertur crudelior ignis? 20
qui natam possis complexu avellere matris,
complexu matris retinentem avellere natam,
et juveni ardenti castam donare puellam.
quid faciunt hostes capta crudelius urbe?
　　Hymen o Hymenaee, Hymen ades o Hymenaee! 25

Hespere, quis caelo lucet jucundior ignis?
qui desponsa tua firmes conubia flamma,
quae pepigere viri, pepigerunt ante parentes,
nec junxere prius quam se tuus extulit ardor.
quid datur a divis felici optatius hora? 30
　　Hymen o Hymenaee, Hymen ades o Hymenaee!

Hesperus e nobis, aequales, abstulit unam:
namque suo adventu fert omnibus ille pericla;
nocte timent cuncti, nisi quos aliena petentes,
Hespere, tu radiis properas accendere blandis.
at libet injusta pueris te extollere laude.
quid tum, si laudant, sibi mox quem quisque timebunt?
　　Hymen o Hymenaee, Hymen ades o Hymenaee!

Hespere, te innuptae nunc falso crimine laedunt:
namque tuo adventu vigilat custodia semper;
nocte latent fures, quos idem saepe revertens,
Hespere, mutato comprendis nomine Eoos. 35
at libet innuptis ficto te carpere questu.
quid tum, si carpunt, tacita quem mente requirunt?
　　Hymen o Hymenaee, Hymen ades o Hymenaee!

GIRLS

Hesperus, what crueller star than you rides in the sky?
For you can tear a daughter from her mother's embrace,
from her mother's embrace tear clinging daughter
and give the chaste girl to an ardent youth.
What crueller deed does the foe commit when a city falls?
   Hail, Hymen Hymenaeus! Hymen Hymenaeus, come!

BOYS

Hesperus, what kinder star than you shines in the sky?
For with your flame you confirm the covenant of marriage
which husbands and which parents have earlier agreed
but have not sealed before your fire has risen on high.
What gift of heaven is more desirable than this happy hour?
   Hail, Hymen Hymenaeus! Hymen Hymenaeus, come!

GIRLS

Hesperus, companions, has stolen one of us:
for, whenever he comes, he brings danger to all;
at night all people fear, save those eager to steal, whom
you, Hesperus, with your seductive beams delight to spur on.
But boys love to extol you with undeserved praise.
What boots their praise, if soon they each shall fear you?
   Hail, Hymen Hymenaeus! Hymen Hymenaeus, come!

BOYS

Hesperus, now the maidens slander you with false charges:
for, whenever you come, watchmen keep constant vigil;
at night thieves lurk, whom many a time you catch,
Hesperus, returning with your name changed to morning star.
But maidens love to carp at you with feigned complaints.
What boots their carping, if secretly within they seek you?
   Hail, Hymen Hymenaeus! Hymen Hymenaeus, come!

Ut flos qui in saeptis secretus nascitur hortis,
ignotus pecori, nullo convulsus aratro,   40
quem mulcent aurae, firmat sol, educat imber,
jam jam se expandit suavesque exspirat odores;
multi illum pueri, multae optavere puellae:
idem cum tenui carptus defloruit ungui,
nulli illum pueri, nullae optavere puellae:
sic virgo, dum intacta manet, dum cara suis est;   45
cum castum amisit polluto corpore florem,
nec pueris jucunda manet, nec cara puellis.
    Hymen o Hymenaee, Hymen ades o Hymenaee!

Ut vidua in nudo vitis quae nascitur arvo,
numquam se extollit, numquam mitem educat uvam,   50
sed tenerum prono deflectens pondere corpus
jam jam contingit summum radice flagellum;
hanc nulli agricolae, nulli coluere juvenci:
at si forte eademst ulmo conjuncta marita,
multi illam agricolae, multi coluere juvenci: 55
sic virgo dum intacta manet, dum inculta senescit;
cum par conubium maturo tempore adeptast,
cara viro magis et minus est invisa parenti.

et tu ne pugna cum tali conjuge, virgo.
non aequumst pugnare, pater cui tradidit ipse,   60
ipse pater cum matre, quibus parere necessest.
virginitas non tota tuast, ex parte parentumst:
tertia pars patris est, pars est data tertia matri,
tertia sola tuast: noli pugnare duobus,
qui genero sua jura simul cum dote dederunt.   65
    Hymen o Hymenaee, Hymen ades o Hymenaee!

GIRLS

As in a garden close a flower grows in a nook,
unknown to the flock, unscathed by any plough,
which winds caress, sun strengthens, rain draws forth,
and even now it opens up and breathes forth sweet fragrance;
it have many boys, it have many girls desired:
but when nipped by the keen-edged nail it has shed its bloom,
it have no boys, it have no girls desired.
Thus a maiden, while untouched, the while is dear to her kin;
when, her body sullied, she loses the flower of maidenhood,
no longer to boys is she lovely, nor is she dear to girls.

    Hail, Hymen Hymenaeus! Hymen Hymenaeus, come!

BOYS

As the unwedded vine which grows on treeless soil
never rears her head, never brings forth a mellow grape,
but bowing her frail body under the drooping weight
even now touches her roots with her topmost tendril;
her have no farmers, her have no steers tended:
but if perchance she is joined in wedlock to the elm,
then her have many farmers, her many steers have tended.
Thus a maiden, while untouched, the while untended ages;
when in the fullness of time she has gained a fitting match,
more dear is she to husband, less frowned upon by father.
(THE BRIDE APPEARS)
And you, maiden, fight not with such a husband.
You must not fight with him your father gave you to himself,
your father himself with your mother, whom you have to obey.
Your virginity is not all yours, but partly your parents':
a third is your father's, a third is allotted your mother,
and only a third is yours: fight not with two who have given
their rights together with the dowry to their son-in-law.

    Hail, Hymen Hymenaeus! Hymen Hymenaeus, come!

LXIII

Super alta vectus Attis
  celeri rate maria,
Phrygium ut nemus citato
  cupide pede tetigit
adiitque opaca silvis
  redimita loca deae,
stimulatus ibi furenti
  rabie, vagus animi,
devulsit ili acuto
  sibi pondera silice.   5
itaque ut relicta sensit
  sibi membra sine viro,
etiam recente terrae
  sola sanguine maculans,
niveis citata cepit
  manibus leve typanum,
typanum tuum, Cybebe,
  tua, mater, initia,
quatiensque terga tauri
  teneris cava digitis   10
canere haec suis adortast
  tremebunda comitibus:

Attis: a tale of religious fanaticism

Attis borne in speedy vessel
    on the crest of seas profound,
when eagerly with restless foot
    he reached the Phrygian woodland
and entered the dark tree-crowned
    demesne of the goddess,
driven on by raging madness
    and wandering in his mind,
he there cut off the weights
    of his groin with a sharp flint.
And then, realizing that the limbs
    had lost their manhood,
and still staining with fresh blood
    the surface of the ground,
the unmanned one on impulse seized
    with delicate hands the light tambourine,
your tambourine, Cybele,
    your mystic instrument, Mother,
and with soft fingers shaking
    the hollow ox-hide
she thus began a-quivering
    to sing to her companions:

'agite ite ad alta, Gallae,
  Cybeles nemora simul,
simul ite, Dindymenae
  dominae vaga pecora,
aliena quae petentes
  velut exules loca
sectam meam secutae
  duce me mihi comites   15
rapidum salum tulistis
  truculentaque pelagi,
et corpus evirastis
  Veneris nimio odio;
hilarate erae citatis
  erroribus animum.
mora tarda mente cedat:
  simul ite, sequimini
Phrygiam ad domum Cybebes,
  Phrygia ad nemora deae,   20
ubi cymbalum sonat vox,
  ubi tympana reboant,
tibicen ubi canit Phryx
  curvo grave calamo,
ubi capita Maenades vi
  jaciunt hederigerae,
ubi sacra sancta acutis
  ululatibus agitant,
ubi suevit illa divae
  volitare vaga cohors,   25
quo nos decet citatis
  celerare tripudiis.'

simul haec comitibus Attis
  cecinit, notha mulier,
thiasus repente linguis
  trepidantibus ululat,
leve tympanum remugit,
  cava cymbala recrepant,

"Up away together, priestesses,
  to Cybele's forest heights;
away together, you wandering droves
  of our lady of Dindymus,
who, seeking alien
  climes as exiles,
following my rule
  as I led you in my train,
have endured the swift-flowing brine
  and the tantrums of the ocean
and have unmanned your bodies
  in utter revulsion from love.
Gladden our lady's heart
  by your impulsive rovings.
Rid your minds of halting delay.
  Away together, follow me
to the Phrygian shrine of Cybele,
  to the Phrygian groves of the goddess,
where rings the clash of cymbals,
  where the tambourines keep sounding,
where the Phrygian piper plays
  a deep note on his curved reed,
where the ivy-crowned Maenads
  violently toss their heads,
where with shrill shrieks they
  celebrate their inviolate rites,
where the goddess's restless
  company loves to bustle:
thither it befits us to hasten
  with impulsive tripping steps."

When thus to her companions Attis
  had sung, a woman counterfeit,
the band of devotees suddenly
  yells aloud with tumultuous tongues,
again rings the light tambourine,
  again clash the hollow cymbals,

viridem citus adit Idam
　　properante pede chorus.　　　　　　30
furibunda simul anhelans
　　vaga vadit, animam agens,
comitata tympano Attis
　　per opaca nemora dux,
veluti juvenca vitans
　　onus indomita jugi:
rapidae ducem sequuntur
　　Gallae properipedem.
itaque, ut domum Cybebes
　　tetigere lassulae,　　　　　　　　35
nimio e labore somnum
　　capiunt sine Cerere.
piger his labante languore
　　oculos sopor operit;
abit in quiete molli
　　rabidus furor animi.
sed ubi oris aurei Sol
　　radiantibus oculis
lustravit aethera album,
　　sola dura, mare ferum,　　　　　　40
pepulitque noctis umbras
　　vegetis sonipedibus,
ibi Somnus excitam Attin
　　fugiens citus abiit:
trepidante quem recepit
　　dea Pasithea sinu.
ita de quiete molli
　　rapida sine rabie
simul ipsa pectore Attis
　　sua facta recoluit,　　　　　　　45
liquidaque mente vidit
　　sine quis ubique foret,
animo aestuante rursus
　　reditum ad vada tetulit.

and with hurrying foot the swift rout
   makes for leafy Ida.
Forthwith when frenzied, panting,
   aimless, gasping for breath,
Attis tambourine in hand
   rushes ahead through the dark woodlands,
like an unbroken heifer refusing
   the burden of the yoke,
the priestesses hurriedly follow
   their fleet-foot guide.
So it was that, when the weary company
   reached Cybele's abode,
after their extreme efforts they fall
   asleep without tasting food.
Their eyes a dull slumber covers
   with a drowsy tiredness;
to gentle peace gives way
   the feverish fury of their breasts.
But when with radiant eyes
   the golden-visaged Sun
surveyed the clear white sky,
   the solid earth, the restless sea,
and put to rout the shades of night
   with his freshened steeds,
thereupon Sleep took flight
   from the waking Attis and sped off
to the goddess Pasithea, who welcomed
   him to her fluttering bosom.
So when after gentle peace
   and freed from restless frenzy
Attis alone with herself
   reviewed what she had done,
and with clear mind saw
   what she lacked and where she was,
with fevered brain she took
   her return back to the sea.

ibi maria vasta visens
   lacrimantibus oculis,
patriam allocuta maestast
   ita voce miseriter:

'patria o mei creatrix,
   patria o mea genetrix,   50
ego quam miser relinquens,
   dominos ut erifugae
famuli solent, ad Idae
   tetuli nemora pedem,
ut apud nivem et ferarum
   gelida stabula forem,
et earum operta adirem
   furibunda latibula,
ubinam aut quibus locis te
   positam, patria, reor?   55
cupit ipsa pupula ad te
   sibi derigere aciem,
rabie fera carens dum
   breve tempus animus est.
egone a mea remota haec
   ferar in nemora domo?
patria, bonis, amicis,
   genitoribus abero?
abero foro, palaestra,
   stadio et gyminasiis?   60
miser ah miser, querendumst
   etiam atque etiam, anime.
quod enim genus figuraest,
   ego non quod obierim?
ego puber, ego adulescens,
   ego ephebus, ego puer,
ego gymnasi fui flos,
   ego eram decus olei:

There as with tear-filled eyes
   she beheld the vastness of the waters,
in deep sadness she addressed
   to her country this pitiful complaint:

"O my country that gave me being,
   O my country that gave me birth,
whom I, a man ill-starred, deserted
   as runaway servants desert
their masters, and to Ida's
   woodlands have I brought my steps,
to dwell amid snow and
   the icy haunts of beasts
and to draw near their hidden
   lairs in my crazed state,
where and in what quarter am I to think,
   my country, that I shall find you?
My eye unbidden longs
   to direct its gaze upon you,
while for a brief moment my mind
   is free from its wild frenzy.
Am I to be carried off to these
   woodlands far from my home?
To be lost to country, possessions,
   friends, and parents?
To be lost to market-place, wrestling-school,
   racetrack, and playground?
Ah, sorry, sorry heart, again and
   yet again must complaint be made.
For what kind of comely figure
   is there which I have not filled?
I have been a grown-up male,
   adolescent, youth, and boy;
I have been the glory of the playground,
   I was the idol of the arena:

mihi januae frequentes,
   mihi limina tepida, 65
mihi floridis corollis
   redimita domus erat,
linquendum ubi esset orto
   mihi sole cubiculum.
ego nunc deum ministra et
   Cybeles famula ferar?
ego Maenas, ego mei pars,
   ego vir sterilis ero?
ego viridis algida Idae
   nive amicta loca colam? 70
ego vitam agam sub altis
   Phrygiae columinibus,
ubi cerva silvicultrix,
   ubi aper nemorivagus?
jam jam dolet quod egi,
   jam jamque paenitet.'

roseis ut huic labellis
   sonitus citus abiit,
dominae deorum ad aures
   nova nuntia referens, 75
ibi juncta juga resolvens
   Cybele leonibus
laevumque pecoris hostem
   stimulans ita loquitur.
'agedum,' inquit 'age ferox i,
   fac ut hanc furor agitet,
fac uti furoris ictu
   reditum in nemora ferat,
mea libere nimis quae
   fugere imperia cupit. 80
age caede terga cauda,
   tua verbera patere,

mine were the thronging doors,
   mine the warm thresholds,
mine the house
   decked with floral wreaths
when, as the sun rose,
   it was time to leave my room.
Am I now to be called a temple servant
   and a handmaid of Cybele?
Am I to be a Maenad,
   but half myself, a barren man?
Am I to haunt the icy snow-clad
   regions of leafy Ida,
and pass my life beneath
   the lofty peaks of Phrygia,
where the forest-haunting hind dwells,
   where the woodland-ranging boar?
Now, now I rue my action,
   now, now do I repent."

  As the utterance swiftly
   issued from her rosy lips,
bringing to the ears of heaven's mistress
   a change of message,
Cybele forthwith loosens
   the fastened yoke from her lions
and, goading the cattle-killer
   who drew on the left, speaks thus.
"Up, up, fierce one," she tells him,
   "go see that frenzy drives her on,
see that under the onset of frenzy
   she makes her return to the woodlands,
she who would be too free and
   desires to escape my sovereignty.
Come, lash your back with your tail,
   endure your self-inflicted blows,

fac cuncta mugienti
  fremitu loca retonent,
rutilam ferox torosa
  cervice quate jubam.'
ait haec minax Cybebe
  religatque juga manu.
ferus ipse sese adhortans
  rabidum incitat animum,   85
vadit, fremit, refringit
  virgulta pede vago.
at ubi umida albicantis
  loca litoris adiit,
teneramque vidit Attin
  prope marmora pelagi,
facit impetum. illa demens
  fugit in nemora fera:
ibi semper omne vitae
  spatium famula fuit.   90

  dea, magna dea, Cybebe,
    dea, domina Dindymi,
procul a mea tuus sit
    furor omnis, era, domo:
alios age incitatos,
    alios age rabidos.

see that all around reverberates
   with bellowing roar,
shake fiercely on sinewy neck
   your ruddy mane."
So speaks Cybele in anger;
   and her hand unbinds the yoke.
Goading himself on the monster
   rouses his soul to fury;
he rushes, he roars, he tramples
   the brushwood in his wild career.
But when he came to the watery wastes
   of the surf-white shore
and saw the unmanned Attis
   by the marble-topped ocean,
he charges. Blind with terror
   she flees into the wild woodlands,
and there evermore for all life's
   course remained a handmaid.

  Goddess, great goddess, Cybele,
   goddess, lady of Dindymus,
far from my house be
   all your fury, queen:
others to that frenzy summon,
   others to that madness drive!

LXIV

Peliaco quondam prognatae vertice pinus
dicuntur liquidas Neptuni nasse per undas
Phasidos ad fluctus et fines Aeeteos,
cum lecti juvenes, Argivae robora pubis,
auratam optantes Colchis avertere pellem   5
ausi sunt vada salsa cita decurrere puppi,
caerula verrentes abjegnis aequora palmis.
diva quibus retinens in summis urbibus arces
ipsa levi fecit volitantem flamine currum,
pinea conjungens inflexae texta carinae.   10
illa rudem cursu prima imbuit Amphitriten.
quae simul ac rostro ventosum proscidit aequor,
tortaque remigio spumis incanuit unda,
emersere freti candenti e gurgite vultus
aequoreae monstrum Nereides admirantes.   15
illa, haud ante alia, viderunt luce marinas
mortales oculis nudato corpore Nymphas
nutricum tenus exstantes e gurgite cano.
tum Thetidis Peleus incensus fertur amore,
tum Thetis humanos non despexit hymenaeos,   20
tum Thetidi pater ipse jugandum Pelea sensit.

o nimis optato saeclorum tempore nati
heroes, salvete, deum genus! o bona matrum
progenies, salvete iterum, salvete, bonarum!   23b
vos ego saepe mero, vos carmine compellabo.
teque adeo, eximie taedis felicibus aucte,   25
Thessaliae columen, Peleu, cui Juppiter ipse,
ipse suos divum genitor concessit amores—
tene Thetis tenuit pulcherrima Nereine,
tene suam Tethys concessit ducere neptem,
Oceanusque, mari totum qui amplectitur orbem?   30

The marriage of Peleus and Thetis

LOVE-MATCH IN THE HEROIC AGE

Pine trees that grew upon Pelion's peak, men say,
floated once long ago through Neptune's watery waves
to the stream of Phasis and Aeetes' realms,
when chosen warriors, the flower of the Argive youth,
eager to carry off from the Colchians the fleece of gold,
ventured in a swift ship to speed over the briny seas
sweeping with blades of fir the azure plains.
For them the goddess who guards the forts on city-tops
with her own hand made a car to fly before the light breeze,
wedding frame of pine to curving keel. That ship was
first to acquaint unschooled Amphitrite with sailing.
As soon as it ploughed with its beak the windy plain,
and, churned by oars, the waves grew white with foam,
forth from the whitening waters of the deep the marine
Nereids lifted their faces in wonder at the sight.
On that and on no earlier dawn did mortal eyes
behold the unclad bodies of ocean nymphs
rising breast-high above the gleaming main.
Then for Thetis was Peleus inflamed with love, 'tis told,
then did Thetis not disdain marriage with a mortal,
then to Thetis the Father perceived must Peleus be yoked.

THE POET SALUTES THE HEROES OF OLD

O born in that too, too happy age of time,
hail, heroes, progeny of gods! O noble sons
of mothers noble, hail and hail again!
You shall I oft toast with wine, you toast with song.
Yes, and you, Peleus, pillar of Thessaly, beyond others
blessed with happy nuptial torch, to whom even Jupiter,
even the king of the gods, resigned his own beloved,—
was it you whom Thetis, fairest of Nereids, embraced,
was it you whom Tethys allowed to wed her daughter's child,
Tethys with Ocean, who encircles the whole earth with sea?

quis simul optatae finito tempore luces
advenere, domum conventu tota frequentat
Thessalia, oppletur laetanti regia coetu:
dona ferunt prae se, declarant gaudia vultu.
deseritur Cieros, linquunt Pthiotica Tempe   35
Crannonisque domos ac moenia Larisaea,
Pharsalum coeunt, Pharsalia tecta frequentant.
rura colit nemo, mollescunt colla juvencis,
non humilis curvis purgatur vinea rastris,
non falx attenuat frondatorum arboris umbram,   41
non glebam prono convellit vomere taurus,   40
squalida desertis robigo infertur aratris.
ipsius at sedes, quacumque opulenta recessit
regia, fulgenti splendent auro atque argento.
candet ebur soliis, collucent pocula mensae,   45
tota domus gaudet regali splendida gaza.
pulvinar vero divae geniale locatur
sedibus in mediis, Indo quod dente politum
tincta tegit roseo conchyli purpura fuco.

haec vestis priscis hominum variata figuris   50
heroum mira virtutes indicat arte.
namque fluentisono prospectans litore Diae,
Thesea cedentem celeri cum classe tuetur
indomitos in corde gerens Ariadna furores,
necdum etiam sese quae visit visere credit,   55
utpote fallaci quae tum primum excita somno
desertam in sola miseram se cernat harena.
immemor at juvenis fugiens pellit vada remis,
irrita ventosae linquens promissa procellae.
quem procul ex alga maestis Minois ocellis,   60
saxea ut effigies bacchantis, prospicit, eheu,
prospicit et magnis curarum fluctuat undis,
non flavo retinens subtilem vertice mitram,
non contecta levi velatum pectus amictu,

ALL THESSALY COMES TO THE WEDDING

When at the appointed time the day they longed for
arrived, all Thessaly with its assembly throngs
the house, the palace is filled with happy company: gifts
they bring in their hands, joy they declare in their faces.
Cieros is deserted; they leave Phthiotic Tempe
and Crannon's homes and the walls of Larissa;
Pharsalus they flock to, Pharsalian halls they throng.
None tends the country, soft grow the necks of steers,
no trailing vine is cleared with curve-pronged rake,
no pruner's hook thins out the shade of trees,
no bull cleaves the sod with deep-driven share,
and scales of rust steal over the abandoned plough.
But the king's own abode, as far inward as stretched the
sumptuous palace, blazes with lustre of gold and silver.
Ivory gleams on the thrones, the cups on the table sparkle,
the whole house rejoices in the splendour of regal wealth.
But the sacred marriage-couch of the goddess is placed
in the midst of the mansion, fashioned of smooth Indic tusk
and covered with purple dyed with the shell's rosy stain.

TABLEAU: ARIADNE ON NAXOS

This coverlet, embroidered with the figures of men of old,
illustrates with wondrous art the brave deeds of heroes.
For, looking forth from the wave-sounding shores of Dia,
Ariadne sees Theseus departing with his swift craft,
nursing in her heart uncontrollable fury;
nor as yet can she believe she beholds what she does behold:
no wonder, since then first she woke from treacherous sleep
and saw herself, poor thing, abandoned on a lonely strand.
But the youth fleeing unmindful of her beats the waters
with his oars, leaving his vain vows to the blustering gale.
Whom Minos' daughter with sad eyes, afar from the weedy
shore, like a Bacchant in marble, looks on, alas,
looks on and is tossed upon great waves of emotion,
not retaining on fair head her fine-spun snood,
not leaving her bosom veiled by gossamer robe,

non tereti strophio lactentes vincta papillas, 65
omnia quae toto delapsa e corpore passim
ipsius ante pedes fluctus salis alludebant.
sed neque tum mitrae neque tum fluitantis amictus
illa vicem curans toto ex te pectore, Theseu,
toto animo, tota pendebat perdita mente. 70
ah misera, assiduis quam luctibus exsternavit
spinosas Erycina serens in pectore curas
illa ex tempestate, ferox quo tempore Theseus
egressus curvis a litoribus Piraei
attigit injusti regis Gortynia tecta. 75

nam perhibent olim crudeli peste coactam
Androgeoneae poenas exsolvere caedis
electos juvenes simul et decus innuptarum
Cecropiam solitam esse dapem dare Minotauro.
quis angusta malis cum moenia vexarentur, 80
ipse suum. Theseus pro caris corpus Athenis
proicere optavit potius quam talia Cretam
funera Cecropiae nec funera portarentur.
atque ita nave levi nitens ac lenibus auris
magnanimum ad Minoa venit sedesque superbas. 85
hunc simul ac cupido conspexit lumine virgo
regia, quam suaves exspirans castus odores
lectulus in molli complexu matris alebat,
quales Eurotae progignunt flumina myrtus
aurave distinctos educit verna colores, 90
non prius ex illo flagrantia declinavit
lumina, quam cuncto concepit corpore flammam
funditus atque imis exarsit tota medullis.
heu misere exagitans immiti corde furores,
sancte puer, curis hominum qui gaudia misces, 95
quaeque regis Golgos quaeque Idalium frondosum,
qualibus incensam jactastis mente puellam
fluctibus, in flavo saepe hospite suspirantem!
quantos illa tulit languenti corde timores!

not keeping her swelling breasts bound by the smooth band:
all these garments, from all her body fallen here and there,
before their mistress's feet the salt waves lapped.
But troubling not then for floating snood, not then
for robe, with all her heart she hung upon you, Theseus,
with all her soul, with all her mind, love-lorn.
Unhappy girl, whom the Lady of Eryx drove out of her senses
with incessant grief, sowing thorny sorrows in her heart
ever since the time when bold Theseus,
departing from the winding shores of the Piraeus,
reached the Cretan palace of the lawless king.

ARIADNE FALLS IN LOVE WITH THESEUS

For they tell how of old, driven by cruel pestilence
to make reparation for the killing of Androgeon,
Cecrops' land used to offer as a feast for the Minotaur her
choicest youths and therewith the flower of her maidenhood.
Now when his little town was sorely pressed by this curse,
Theseus himself for his own dear Athens chose rather
to hazard his life than that to Crete such
living corpses from Cecrops' land be freighted.
Thus then, speeding in a light ship before gentle winds,
he came to lordly Minos and his palace proud.
As soon as with longing eyes the king's daughter beheld him,
she whom her maiden bed, breathing sweet odours,
still nursed in her mother's soft embrace, odours as of
myrtles reared by the waters of Eurotas or flowers
of varied hue coaxed into bloom by breath of spring,
she turned not her burning glance away from him
until she caught fire in all her frame
deep within and totally burned to her inmost marrow.
Alas, you, who with cruel heart wretchedly excite passions,
divine boy, who mix together human joys and sorrows,
and you, queen, who rule Golgi and leafy Idalium,
upon what billows ye tossed that soul-kindled maiden
as she oft sighed for the golden-haired stranger!
What fears she suffered with fainting heart!

quam tum saepe magis fulgore expalluit auri,   100
cum saevum cupiens contra contendere monstrum
aut mortem appeteret Theseus aut praemia laudis!
non ingrata tamen frustra munuscula divis
promittens tacito suscepit vota labello.
nam velut in summo quatientem bracchia Tauro   105
quercum aut conigeram sudanti cortice pinum
indomitus turbo contorquens flamine robur
eruit (illa procul radicitus exturbata
prona cadit, late quaecumque habet obvia frangens),
sic domito saevum prostravit corpore Theseus   110
nequiquam vanis jactantem cornua ventis.
inde pedem sospes multa cum laude reflexit
errabunda regens tenui vestigia filo,
ne labyrintheis e flexibus egredientem
tecti frustraretur inobservabilis error.   115

sed quid ego a primo digressus carmine plura
commemorem, ut linquens genitoris filia vultum,
ut consanguineae complexum, ut denique matris,
quae misera in nata deperdita lamentatast,
omnibus his Thesei dulcem praeoptarit amorem,   120
aut ut vecta rati spumosa ad litora Diae
venerit, aut ut eam devinctam lumina somno
liquerit immemori discedens pectore conjunx?
saepe illam perhibent ardenti corde furentem
clarisonas imo fudisse e pectore voces,   125
ac tum praeruptas tristem conscendere montes,
unde aciem in pelagi vastos protenderet aestus,
tum tremuli salis adversas procurrere in undas
mollia nudatae tollentem tegmine surae,
atque haec extremis maestam dixisse querellis,   130
frigidulos udo singultus ore cientem:
'sicine me patriis avectam, perfide, ab aris,
perfide, deserto liquisti in litore, Theseu?
sicine discedens neglecto numine divum

How oft did she then grow paler than gold's bright paleness,
when, eager to contend with the savage monster,
Theseus sought either death or the prize of glory!
Not unpleasing however or in vain were the gifts she pledged
the gods, when with silent lips she framed her vow.
For just as an oak that shakes its arms on Taurus' heights
or a cone-bearing pine with resinous bark is torn up by an
irresistible tornado which twists the trunk with its blast:
dislodged, roots and all, the tree falls prone afar,
smashing over a wide area all it finds in its way:
so, overpowering its bulk, did Theseus lay low the monster
as it vainly tossed its horns at the empty air.
Thence unharmed and with much renown he retraced his path,
guiding with slender thread his steps that else would stray,
lest, as he sought to emerge from the labyrinthine windings,
the building's untraceable maze baffle him.

ARIADNE'S SOLILOQUY

But why wander from my first theme and tell of more?
How the daughter forsook the sight of her father,
how forsook her sister's, how even mother's embrace,
who over her ill-starred child wept inconsolably,
and preferred to all of these the dear love of Theseus?
Or how, a passenger on ship, she came to Dia's foaming
shores, or how when her eyes were locked in sleep she was
forsaken by a husband who departed with forgetful mind?
Oft, they say, in the fury of her burning heart she
poured forth piercing cries from the depths of her being;
and now she would sorrowfully climb the precipitous cliffs,
from which to extend her gaze over the vast swell of ocean,
now run out into the incoming waves of the restless sea,
lifting high her bared ankles' soft coverings;
and these words she sadly uttered in her last laments,
heaving shivering sobs with tear-stained face:
'Thus, faithless one, having lured me from my ancestral altar,
faithless Theseus, have you left me on a desolate shore?
Thus, indifferent to the will of heaven, do you depart

immemor ah devota domum perjuria portas?   135
nullane res potuit crudelis flectere mentis
consilium? tibi nulla fuit clementia praesto,
immite ut nostri vellet miserescere pectus?
at non haec quondam blanda promissa dedisti
voce mihi, non haec miseram sperare jubebas,   140
sed conubia laeta, sed optatos hymenaeos;
quae cuncta aerii discerpunt irrita venti.
nunc jam nulla viro juranti femina credat,
nulla viri speret sermones esse fideles;
quis dum aliquid cupiens animus praegestit apisci,   145
nil metuunt jurare, nihil promittere parcunt:
sed simul ac cupidae mentis satiata libidost,
dicta nihil meminere, nihil perjuria curant.
certe ego te in medio versantem turbine leti
eripui, et potius germanum amittere crevi,   150
quam tibi fallaci supremo in tempore dessem.
pro quo dilaceranda feris dabor alitibusque
praeda, neque injecta tumulabor mortua terra.
quaenam te genuit sola sub rupe leaena,
quod mare conceptum spumantibus exspuit undis,   155
quae Syrtis, quae Scylla rapax, quae vasta Charybdis,
talia qui reddis pro dulci praemia vita?
si tibi non cordi fuerant conubia nostra,
saeva quod horrebas prisci praecepta parentis,
attamen in vestras potuisti ducere sedes,   160
quae tibi jucundo famularer serva labore,
candida permulcens liquidis vestigia lymphis,
purpureave tuum consternens veste cubile.
sed quid ego ignaris nequiquam conqueror auris,
exsternata malo, quae nullis sensibus auctae   165
nec missas audire queunt nec reddere voces?
ille autem prope jam mediis versatur in undis,
nec quisquam apparet vacua mortalis in alga.
sic, nimis insultans extremo tempore saeva,
fors etiam nostris invidit questibus aures.   170

and ah, unmindful, carry home the curse upon your broken oath?
Could nothing deflect the purpose of your cruel
mind? Was no compassion present in your soul
to prompt that ruthless heart to take pity on me?
But not such were the promises you gave me once with winning
words, not such the hopes you bade me, poor fool, conceive,
but happy wedlock and the nuptials I longed for;
all which the winds of the air have shredded into nothingness.
Henceforth let no woman believe a man's oaths,
nor in a man's speeches look for loyalty;
for while their desirous hearts crave to obtain something,
no oath they fear to swear, no promise they forbear to make:
but once the lust of their desirous minds is gratified,
no remembrance have they of words, no regard for perjuries.
I rescued you, as you know well, when whirled in death's
inmost eddy, and rather chose to sacrifice a brother
than to fail you, now found faithless, in your hour of need.
For this I shall be given as prey to bird and beast to rend,
nor secure when dead the burial of a scattering of earth.
What lioness bore you beneath some solitary rock,
what sea conceived and vomited you from its foaming waters,
what Syrtis, what ravening Scylla, what monstrous Charybdis,
you who for precious life have given such return?
If marriage with me had not been to your pleasure,
because you dreaded the cruel edicts of a severe father,
yet at least you could have brought me to your house
to be your slave and serve you as a labour of love,
bathing your bright feet with water from the spring
or spreading the purple coverlet upon your bed.
But why, besides myself with woe, do I make vain complaint
to the unfeeling breezes, which, unendowed with sense,
can neither hear words uttered nor give them in reply?
By now, however, he must be nigh midway on his course,
and still not a soul is to be seen upon the empty beach.
Thus all too spiteful, mocking me in my hour of agony,
has fortune grudged even a listener to my complaints.

Juppiter omnipotens, utinam ne tempore primo
Cnosia Cecropiae tetigissent litora puppes,
indomito nec dira ferens stipendia tauro
perfidus intortum religasset navita funem,
nec malus haec celans dulci crudelia forma   175
consilia in nostris requiesset sedibus hospes!
nam quo me referam? quali spe perdita nitor?
Idaeosne petam montes? at gurgite lato
discernens ponti truculentum dividit aequor.
an patris auxilium sperem? quemne ipse reliqui   180
respersum juvenem fraterna caede secuta?
conjugis an fido consoler memet amore?
quine fugit lentos incurvans gurgite remos?
praeterea nullo colitur sola insula tecto,
nec patet egressus pelagi cingentibus undis.   185
nulla fugae ratio, nullast spes: omnia muta,
omnia sunt deserta, ostentant omnia letum.
non tamen ante mihi languescent lumina morte,
nec prius a fesso secedent corpore sensus,
quam justam a divis exposcam prodita multam,   190
caelestumque fidem postrema comprecer hora.
quare, facta virum multantes vindice poena,
Eumenides, quibus anguino redimita capillo
frons exspirantes praeportat pectoris iras,
huc huc adventate, meas audite querellas,   195
quas ego, vae misera, extremis proferre medullis
cogor inops, ardens, amenti caeca furore.
quae quoniam verae nascuntur pectore ab imo,
vos nolite pati nostrum vanescere luctum,
sed quali solam Theseus me mente reliquit,   200
tali mente, deae, funestet seque suosque.'

has postquam maesto profudit pectore voces,
supplicium saevis exposcens anxia factis,
adnuit invicto caelestum numine rector;
quo motu tellus atque horrida contremuerunt   205

Almighty Jupiter, would that in the beginning
Athenian ships had not reached Cnossian shores,
nor, bearing the dreadful tribute to the savage bull,
had the faithless seaman tied up his twisted cable,
nor had villainously, concealing under a mask of beauty
these cruel designs, sojourned in our home, a guest!
Just where am I to turn? On what hope do I lean, abandoned?
Make for the mountains of Crete? But barring them with
wide expanse the stormy waters of the sea lie in between.
Hope for father's help, the father I wilfully deserted,
chasing after a youth stained with my brother's blood?
Console myself with the faithful love of a husband, one who,
bending his pliant oars in the deep, is fleeing from me?
Besides, the island is remote, unoccupied by any dwelling,
and with ocean's waves about it no escape is possible.
There is no means of flight, no hope: all around is silent,
all is desolate, all presents the face of doom.
Yet shall my eyes not droop in death
nor sense depart from my fainting body
before from the gods I demand full penalty for my betrayal
and in my last moments appeal for heaven's justice.
Wherefore, ye Furies, who punish men's deeds with vengeful
penalty, whose forehead, crowned with snaky locks,
proclaims the blast of anger from your hearts,
come hither and hearken to my complaints, which I
poor wretch, am forced to utter from my inmost heart,
helpless, burning, blinded with raging frenzy. And
since they are just and spring from the bottom of my soul,
suffer not my anguish to come to naught,
but in what forgetfulness Theseus left me forlorn,
even in that, O goddesses, may he ruin himself and his.'
THE FORGETFULNESS OF THESEUS
When from her sad soul she had poured forth this utterance,
earnestly imploring vengeance for such cruel deeds,
the ruler of the gods bowed assent with sovereign nod;
and at the movement the earth and ruffled waters

aequora concussitque micantia sidera mundus.
ipse autem caeca mentem caligine Theseus
consitus oblito dimisit pectore cuncta,
quae mandata prius constanti mente tenebat,
dulcia nec maesto sustollens signa parenti   210
sospitem Erectheum se ostendit visere portum.
namque ferunt olim, classi cum moenia divae
linquentem natum ventis concrederet Aegeus,
talia complexum juveni mandata dedisse:
'nate mihi longe jucundior unice vita,   215
reddite in extrema nuper mihi fine senectae,   217
nate, ego quem in dubios cogor dimittere casus,   216
quandoquidem fortuna mea ac tua fervida virtus
eripit invito mihi te, cui languida nondum
lumina sunt nati cara saturata figura,   220
non ego te gaudens laetanti pectore mittam,
nec te ferre sinam fortunae signa secundae,
sed primum multas expromam mente querellas,
canitiem terra atque infuso pulvere foedans,
inde infecta vago suspendam lintea malo,   225
nostros ut luctus nostraeque incendia mentis
carbasus obscurata decet ferrugine Hibera.
quod tibi si sancti concesserit incola Itoni,
quae nostrum genus ac sedes defendere Erecthei
adnuit, ut tauri respergas sanguine dextram,   230
tum vero facito ut memori tibi condita corde
haec vigeant mandata, nec ulla oblitteret aetas;
ut, simul ac nostros invisent lumina colles,
funestam antemnae deponant undique vestem,
candidaque intorti sustollant vela rudentes,   235
quam primum cernens ut laeta gaudia mente
agnoscam, cum te reducem fors prospera sistet.'
haec mandata prius constanti mente tenentem
Thesea ceu pulsae ventorum flamine nubes
aerium nivei montis liquere cacumen.   240
at pater, ut summa prospectum ex arce petebat,

trembled, and the firmament shook its twinkling stars.
But Theseus himself, his mind sown thick with blinding
darkness, let go from his forgetful heart all the charge
to which he had hitherto held fast with constant purpose,
and hoisted not the glad signal for his grieving father
to announce his safe return to Erechtheus' harbour.
For they say that earlier, when entrusting to the winds
his son, as in his craft he left the goddess's walls,
Aegeus embraced the youth and gave him this charge:
'Son, only son, sweeter by far to me than life itself,
restored to me but now at the extreme limit of old age,
son, whom I am forced to let go on perilous ventures,
since my lot and your burning valour
tear you from me in my despite, for not yet have
my failing eyes feasted enough on my son's dear face,
not as one glad with joyous heart will I send you forth,
nor let you bear the flag of happy fortune,
but first will I fetch forth from my soul many a lament,
soiling my grey hairs with sprinkled dust of earth,
and then will I hang blackened sails upon your errant mast,
seeing that canvas stained with Spanish dye befits
the fire of grief that consumes my soul.
But if she who dwells in holy Itonus, she who
vouchsafes to defend our people and Erechtheus' home,
grants you to steep your hand in the blood of the Minotaur,
then be sure that, stored in a mindful heart, this
charge retains its freshness, undulled by lapse of time,
so that, as soon as your eyes catch sight of our hills,
the yards drop everywhere their garb of mourning
and the twisted ropes hoist white sails,
that with all speed I may see and welcome with joyful heart
the glad tidings, when a happy lot brings you safely back.'
This charge, though kept at first with constant purpose,
left Theseus' mind, as clouds driven by the blast of winds
leave the airy crest of a snow-capped mountain.
But his father, as he scanned the view from the top of the

anxia in assiduos absumens lumina fletus,
cum primum infecti conspexit lintea veli,
praecipitem sese scopulorum e vertice jecit,
amissum credens immiti Thesea fato.   245
sic, funesta domus ingressus tecta paterna
morte, ferox Theseus, qualem Minoidi luctum
obtulerat mente immemori, talem ipse recepit.
quae tum prospectans cedentem maesta carinam
multiplices animo volvebat saucia curas.   250

at parte ex alia florens volitabat Iacchus
cum thiaso Satyrorum et Nysigenis Silenis,
te quaerens, Ariadna, tuoque incensus amore.
cui Thyades passim lymphata mente furebant
euhoe bacchantes, euhoe capita inflectentes.   255
harum pars tecta quatiebant cuspide thyrsos,
pars e divulso jactabant membra juvenco,
pars sese tortis serpentibus incingebant,
pars obscura cavis celebrabant orgia cistis,
orgia quae frustra cupiunt audire profani;   260
plangebant aliae proceris tympana palmis,
aut tereti tenues tinnitus aere ciebant;
multis raucisonos efflabant cornua bombos,
barbaraque horribili stridebat tibia cantu.
talibus amplifice vestis decorata figuris   265
pulvinar complexa suo velabat amictu.

quae postquam cupide spectando Thessala pubes
expletast, sanctis coepit decedere divis.
hic, qualis flatu placidum mare matutino
horrificans Zephyrus proclivas incitat undas   270
Aurora exoriente vagi sub limina Solis,
quae tarde primum clementi flamine pulsae
procedunt leviterque sonant plangore cachinni,
post vento crescente magis magis increbrescunt,
purpureaque procul nantes ab luce refulgent: 275

citadel, wasting his anxious eyes in endless weeping,
the moment he descried the canvas of the darkened sail,
hurled himself headlong from the summit of the rocks,
believing Theseus to have perished by a merciless fate.
Thus, as he entered palace-halls which mourned his father's
death, bold Theseus himself encountered such grief as with
forgetful heart he had brought on Minos' daughter.
And she the while, tearfully looking at the receding ship,
was turning over manifold woes heart-stricken.

TABLEAU: BACCHANAL

But elsewhere on the tapestry Iacchus in the bloom of youth
was hastening with his troop of satyrs and Sileni Nysa-born,
seeking you, Ariadne, and inflamed with love of you.
At his bidding Maenads all about were raving frenziedly
crying 'Evoe' in a tumult, 'Evoe' as they tossed their heads.
Of them some were brandishing wands with ivy-covered tips,
some were scattering the limbs of a heifer torn to pieces,
some were girding themselves with writhing snakes,
some were processing with mystic emblems in deep caskets,
emblems which the uninitiated vainly long to learn,
others with uplifted hands were beating on the tambourines
or stirring shrill tinklings on cymbals of rounded bronze;
many were causing horns to blare out hoarse-booming blasts
and the outlandish pipe to scream with a frightening note.
Such were the figures that sumptuously adorned the tapestry
which clasped and clothed the couch with its folds.

THE MORTALS DEPART, THE GODS ARRIVE

When the youth of Thessaly were sated with eager inspection
of these scenes, they began to make way for the holy gods.
Thereupon, just as the Zephyr, ruffling the calm sea
with breeze of morning, rouses the waves to tumble forwards
when Dawn rises up to the portals of the journeying Sun:
at first, uged by a gentle breath, they move in slow
procession, and with soft splash do laughing ripples sound;
then, as the wind freshens, they crowd faster and faster on
and floating far from the rosy light reflect its splendour:

sic tum vestibulo linquentes regia tecta
ad se quisque vago passim pede discedebant.
quorum post abitum princeps a vertice Peli
advenit Chiron portans silvestria dona:
nam quoscumque ferunt campi, quos Thessala magnis   280
montibus ora creat, quos propter fluminis undas
aura aperit flores tepidi fecunda Favoni,
hos indistinctis plexos tulit ipse corollis,
quo permulsa domus jucundo risit odore.
confestim Peneos adest, viridantia Tempe,   285
Tempe, quae silvae cingunt super impendentes,
Haemonisin linquens crebris celebranda choreis,
non vacuus: namque ille tulit radicitus altas
fagos ac recto proceras stipite laurus,
non sine nutanti platano lentaque sorore   290
flammati Phaethontis et aeria cupressu.
haec circum sedes late contexta locavit,
vestibulum ut molli velatum fronde vireret.
post hunc consequitur sollerti corde Prometheus,
extenuata gerens veteris vestigia poenae,   295
quam quondam silici restrictus membra catena
persolvit pendens e verticibus praeruptis.
inde pater divum sancta cum conjuge natisque
advenit, caelo te solum, Phoebe, relinquens
unigenamque simul cultricem montibus Idri: 300
Pelea nam tecum pariter soror aspernatast,
nec Thetidis taedas voluit celebrare jugales.

qui postquam niveis flexerunt sedibus artus,
large multiplici constructae sunt dape mensae,
cum interea infirmo quatientes corpora motu   305
veridicos Parcae coeperunt edere cantus.
his corpus tremulum complectens undique vestis
candida purpurea talos incinxerat ora,
at roseae niveo residebant vertice vittae,
aeternumque manus carpebant rite laborem.   310

so then, leaving by the fore-court the royal abode,
in all directions each went home with divergent steps.
First after their departure came Chiron
from the crest of Pelion, bringing woodland gifts:
for all the flowers the plains bear, all that on its mighty
mountains the land of Thessaly produces, all that by running
waters warm Favonius' fruitful breeze opens into bloom,
these he brought himself twined in unsorted posies,
caressed by whose pleasant fragrance the palace smiles.
Hard on his heels comes Peneus, leaving verdant Tempe,
Tempe crowned with overhanging woods,
for the daughters of Thessaly to fill with thronging dances,
nor comes without a gift: for he comes carrying, roots and
all, giant beeches and tall laurels straight of stem
together with the waving plane-tree, the swaying sister
of blasted Phaethon and the towering cypress.
Around the house he placed a broad screen of these, that
the fore-court might be embowered in soft green foliage.
Him follows Prometheus, he of the inventive mind,
bearing the faded scars of the ancient punishment
which, his limbs chained to a rock, he once
endured, hanging upon a precipitous peak. Then came the
father of the gods with his august spouse and his children,
leaving in heaven only you, Phoebus, and with you your
twin sister, hauntress of the heights of Idrus:
for no less than you your sister scorned Peleus
and wished not to attend the nuptial rites of Thetis.

THE FATES SING AN EPITHALAMIUM

After they had folded their limbs on the ivory seats,
the tables were piled abundantly with various viands,
and meanwhile, their frames shaking with palsied gesture,
the Fates began to utter truth-telling chants.
A white garment, completely wrapping their feeble limbs,
circled their ankles with its crimson fringe,
whilst on their hoary crowns sat rosy ribbons,
as their hands solemnly plied their never-ending task.

laeva colum molli lana retinebat amictum,
dextera tum leviter deducens fila supinis
formabat digitis, tum prono in pollice torquens
libratum tereti versabat turbine fusum,
atque ita decerpens aequabat semper opus dens,   315
laneaque aridulis haerebant morsa labellis,
quae prius in levi fuerant exstantia filo:
ante pedes autem candentis mollia lanae
vellera virgati custodibant calathisci.
hae tum clarisona vellentes vellera voce   320
talia divino fuderunt carmine fata,
carmine, perfidiae quod post nulla arguet aetas.

o decus eximium magnis virtutibus augens,
Emathiae tutamen, Opis carissime nato,
accipe, quod laeta tibi pandunt luce sorores,   325
veridicum oraclum: sed vos, quae fata sequuntur,
    currite ducentes subtegmina, currite, fusi.

adveniet tibi jam portans optata maritis
Hesperus, adveniet fausto cum sidere conjunx,
quae tibi flexanimo mentem perfundat amore,   330
languidulosque paret tecum conjungere somnos,
levia substernens robusto bracchia collo.
    currite ducentes subtegmina, currite, fusi.

nulla domus tales umquam contexit amores,
nullus amor tali conjunxit foedere amantes,   335
qualis adest Thetidi, qualis concordia Peleo.
    currite ducentes subtegmina, currite, fusi.

nascetur vobis expers terroris Achilles,
hostibus haud tergo, sed forti pectore notus,
qui persaepe vago victor certamine cursus   340
flammea praevertet celeris vestigia cervae.
    currite ducentes subtegmina, currite, fusi.

The left hand held the distaff wrapped in soft wool;
the right, drawing the threads lightly down, gave them shape
with upturned fingers, then twisted them on downturned
thumb and twirled the spindle poised by its rounded disc.
And ever as they span, their teeth nipped and smoothed
the work, and to their parched lips clung bitten ends of
wool that before had made a roughness on the even thread.
At their feet the soft fleeces of gleaming wool
were stored in baskets of osier.
Plucking the threads, they then in clear-toned accents
poured forth these prophecies in inspired song,
song that no age hereafter shall convict of falsehood.

'You who with heroic deeds crown high repute,
bulwark of Thessaly, to son of Ops most dear,
receive the truth-telling oracle which on this joyous day
the sisters reveal for you: but drawing the woof-threads,
   on which destiny depends, do you run, spindles, run.

Soon shall come Hesperus, bringing you what bridegrooms
desire, and with the auspicious star shall come your wife
to bathe your heart in soul-charming love,
to haste to share with you soft languors of sleep
putting her delicate arms beneath your manly neck.
   Run, drawing the woof-threads, spindles, run.

No house ever harboured such loves as these,
no love ever joined lovers with such a bond
as is the harmony between Thetis and Peleus.
   Run, drawing the woof-threads, spindles, run.

To you shall be born a son devoid of fear, Achilles,
known to the foe not by his back, but by valiant breast,
who, full often victorious in the far-ranging footrace,
shall outstrip the flame-fleet steps of the swift hind.
   Run, drawing the woof-threads, spindles, run.

non illi quisquam bello se conferet heros,
cum Phrygii Teucro manabunt sanguine campi,
Troicaque obsidens longinquo moenia bello,   345
perjuri Pelopis vastabit tertius heres.
    currite ducentes subtegmina, currite, fusi.

illius egregias virtutes claraque facta
saepe fatebuntur natorum in funere matres,
cum incultum cano solvent a vertice crinem,   350
putridaque infirmis variabunt pectora palmis.
    currite ducentes subtegmina, currite, fusi.

namque velut densas praecerpens messor aristas
sole sub ardenti flaventia demetit arva,
Trojugenum infesto prosternet corpora ferro.   355
    currite ducentes subtegmina, currite, fusi.

testis erit magnis virtutibus unda Scamandri,
quae passim rapido diffunditur Hellesponto,
cujus iter densis angustans corporum acervis
alta tepefaciet permixta flumina caede.   360
    currite ducentes subtegmina, currite, fusi.

denique testis erit morti quoque reddita praeda,
cum teres excelso coacervatum aggere bustum
excipiet niveos perculsae virginis artus.
    currite ducentes subtegmina, currite, fusi.   365

nam simul ac fessis dederit fors copiam Achivis
urbis Dardaniae Neptunia solvere vincla,
alta Polyxenia madefient caede sepulcra;
quae, velut ancipiti succumbens victima ferro,
proiciet truncum summisso poplite corpus.   370
    currite ducentes subtegmina, currite, fusi.

quare agite optatos animi conjungite amores,
accipiant conjunx felici foedere divam,
dedatur cupido jam dudum nupta marito.
    currite ducentes subtegmina, currite, fusi.   375

No champion shall hold his own with him in combat,
when Phrygian plains flow with Trojan blood
and the third in line from perjured Pelops, beleaguering it
in protracted siege, razes the fortress of Troy.
    Run, drawing the woof-threads, spindles, run.

His outstanding exploits and deeds of fame
shall mothers oft acknowledge at the funeral of their sons,
when from their hoary heads they let fall dishevelled locks
and bruise with weak palms their withered breasts.
    Run, drawing the woof-threads, spindles, run.

For as the harvester, lopping the thick ears of corn
beneath the blazing sun, mows down the golden fields, so
shall he with ruthless sword lay low the bodies of Trojans.
    Run, drawing the woof-threads, spindles, run.

His heroic exploits shall be attested by Scamander's stream
which pours diffusely forth into the swirling Hellespont,
whose channel he shall choke with clogging heaps of corpses
and warm the deep stream with mingled gore.
    Run, drawing the woof-threads, spindles, run.

Lastly, they shall be attested by a victim given him
in death, when the rounded tomb heaped into a high barrow
shall receive the snowy limbs of a slaughtered virgin.
    Run, drawing the woof-threads, spindles, run.

For as soon as chance gives the weary Achaeans power
to undo the coronal wrought by Neptune round Dardan's town,
the lofty sepulchre shall be wetted with Polyxena's blood;
and she, like a victim smitten by a two-edged sword,
shall bending her knees fall forward, a headless corpse.
    Run, drawing the woof-threads, spindles, run.

Come therefore and consummate the love your hearts desire.
Let the groom receive the goddess in happy wedlock,
let the bride be forthwith given to her eager spouse.
    Run, drawing the woof-threads, spindles, run.

non illam nutrix orienti luce revisens
hesterno collum poterit circumdare filo,   377
anxia nec mater discordis maesta puellae   379
secubitu caros mittet sperare nepotes.
    currite ducentes subtegmina, currite, fusi.

talia praefantes quondam felicia Peleo
carmina divino cecinerunt pectore Parcae.
praesentes namque ante domos invisere castas
heroum et sese mortali ostendere coetu   385
caelicolae nondum spreta pietate solebant.
saepe pater divum templo in fulgente residens,
annua cum festis venissent sacra diebus,
conspexit terra centum procumbere tauros.
saepe vagus Liber Parnasi vertice summo   390
Thyiadas effusis euhantes crinibus egit,
cum Delphi tota certatim ex urbe ruentes
acciperent laeti divum fumantibus aris.
saepe in letifero belli certamine Mavors
aut rapidi Tritonis era aut Amarynthia virgo   395
armatas hominumst praesens hortata catervas.
sed postquam tellus scelerest imbuta nefando,
justitiamque omnes cupida de mente fugarunt,
perfudere manus fraterno sanguine fratres,
destitit exstinctos natus lugere parentes,   400
optavit genitor primaevi funera nati,
liber uti nuptae poteretur flore novellae,
ignaro mater substernens se improba nato
impia non veritast divos scelerare penates:
omnia fanda nefanda malo permixta furore   405
justificam nobis mentem avertere deorum.
quare nec tales dignantur visere coetus,
nec se contingi patiuntur lumine claro.

When her nurse revisits her at dawn of day, she will not
be able to circle her neck with yesterday's riband,
nor shall her anxious mother, sad at daughter's estrangement
from the marriage-bed, cease to hope for grandchildren.
    Run, drawing the woof-threads, spindles, run.'

THE END OF THE HEROIC AGE

Such strains once long ago, portending happiness for Peleus,
sang the Fates from prophetic breast.
For formerly the gods in bodily shape used to visit
the pious homes of heroes and show themselves
in mortal gatherings when religion was not yet despised.
Oft the father of the gods, enthroned in splendid temple,
when his yearly rites came round with their festal days,
beheld a hundred bullocks crumple to the ground.
Oft roving on the topmost heights of Parnassus did Bacchus
drive his Maenads shrieking with dishevelled hair,
when the Delphians racing eagerly from all the town
joyfully welcomed the god with smoking altars.
Oft in the death-dealing strife of war did Mars
or swift Triton's mistress or the Amarynthian maid
with their presence urge on the armed hosts of men.
But when the earth was steeped in ghastly crime,
and all men banished righteousness from their lustful hearts,
brothers bathed their hands in brothers' blood,
son ceased to mourn his parents' death,
father longed for the death of eldest son,
that he might be free to enjoy a young wife's beauty,
and a wanton mother, coupling with her unwitting son,
feared not, impious wretch, to pollute her family gods:
then the mingling of all right and wrong in sinful madness
turned from us the righteous will of the gods.
Wherefore they deign not to visit such gatherings as ours
nor let themselves be touched by the broad light of day.

LXV

Etsi me assiduo defectum cura dolore
    sevocat a doctis, Hortale, virginibus,
nec potis est dulces Musarum expromere fetus
    mens animi (tantis fluctuat ipsa malis:
namque mei nuper Lethaeo gurgite fratris   5
    pallidulum manans alluit unda pedem,
Troica Rhoeteo quem subter litore tellus
    ereptum nostris obterit ex oculis—
numquam ego te potero posthac audire loquentem,
    numquam ego te, vita frater amabilior,   10
aspiciam posthac? at certe semper amabo,
    semper maesta tua carmina morte canam,
qualia sub densis ramorum concinit umbris
    Daulias, absumpti fata gemens Ityli):
sed tamen in tantis maeroribus, Hortale, mitto   15
    haec expressa tibi carmina Battiadae,
ne tua dicta vagis nequiquam credita ventis
    effluxisse meo forte putes animo,
ut missum sponsi furtivo munere malum
    procurrit casto virginis e gremio,   20
quod miserae oblitae molli sub veste locatum,
    dum adventu matris prosilit, excutitur;
atque illud prono praeceps agitur decursu,
    huic manat tristi conscius ore rubor.

Letter accompanying a translation

Although I am worn out by enduring grief, Hortalus,
    and sorrow keeps me away from the learned maids,
nor can my mind's imagination yield the sweet produce
    of the Muses (on such a sea of troubles is it tossed:
for the creeping tide of Lethe's stream has lately
    washed the death-pale foot of my brother,
on whom torn from my sight the soil of Troy
    lies heavy beneath the Rhoetean shore—
shall I never hereafter be able to hear your voice,
    shall I never hereafter set eyes on you, brother dearer
than life? But have no doubt that I shall always love you,
    always be singing songs saddened by your death,
songs such as in the shade of thick boughs the Daulian bird
    pours forth in lamentation for the death of Itylus):
yet in the midst of such sorrow, Hortalus, I send
    you translated these verses of the Battiad,
in case perchance you fancy that your words were vainly spent
    upon the passing winds and have slipped from my mind,
as an apple, stealthily sent as a gift from her lover,
    rolls out from a chaste maiden's bosom (for she forgets,
poor thing, that it is hidden beneath her soft gown) and is
    shaken out when she starts up at her mother's coming;
and flung headlong it tumbles to the ground,
    while over her sorry face spreads a guilty blush.

LXVI

Omnia qui magni dispexit lumina mundi,
    qui stellarum ortus comperit atque obitus,
flammeus ut rapidi solis nitor obscuretur,
    ut cedant certis sidera temporibus,
ut Triviam furtim sub Latmia saxa relegans   5
    dulcis amor gyro devocet aerio:
idem me ille Conon caelesti in limine vidit
    e Bereniceo vertice caesariem
fulgentem clare, quam cunctis illa deorum
    levia protendens bracchia pollicitast,   10
qua rex tempestate novo auctatus hymenaeo
    vastatum fines iverat Assyrios,
dulcia nocturnae portans vestigia rixae,
    quam de virgineis gesserat exuviis.
estne novis nuptis odio Venus? an quod aventum   15
    frustrantur falsis gaudia lacrimulis,
ubertim thalami quas juxta limina fundunt?
    non, ita me divi, vera gemunt, juerint.
id mea me multis docuit regina querellis
    invisente novo proelia torva viro.   20
et tu non orbum luxti deserta cubile,
    sed fratris cari flebile discidium?
quam penitus maestas exedit cura medullas!
    ut tibi tunc toto pectore sollicitae
sensibus ereptis mens excidit! at te ego certe   25
    cognoram a parva virgine magnanimam.
anne bonum oblita's facinus, quo regium adepta's
    conjugium, quo non fortius ausit alis?
sed tum maesta virum mittens quae verba locuta's!
    Juppiter, ut tersti lumina saepe manu!   30

The Lock of Berenice

He who discerned all the luminaries of the mighty firmament,
    who computed the risings and the settings of the stars,
how the fiery splendour of the scorching sun is eclipsed,
    how the constellations depart at appointed seasons,
how sweet love calls down the Moon from her orbit on high,
    banishing her secretly to the rocky cave of Latmos—
that same Conon espied me shining brightly upon the floor
    of heaven, me a lock from the head of Berenice,
whom she, stretching forth her smooth arms,
    promised to the whole company of the gods
at the time that, blessed with recent marriage, the king
    went forth to harry the Assyrian borders,
bearing the sweet scars of the nocturnal struggle
    he had waged to win the spoil of her virginity.
Is Venus hated by brides? Or is it that they mock
    the joys of eager grooms with tears that are feigned,
those tears they shed so freely at the bedroom door?
    Theirs, so help me heaven, is no real grief.
This my queen taught me by her many lamentations
    when her bridegroom embarked on savage war.
And you wept, you say, not as deserted wife for widowed bed,
    but for the sad separation from a dear brother?
How utterly did anguish consume your unhappy soul!
    How then your whole heart was troubled, and
bereft of your senses you fainted! And yet, to be sure,
    I knew you from early girlhood to be courageous.
Or have you forgotten the noble deed whereby you won a royal
    marriage? No braver deed could another dare. But then,
sadly letting your husband go, what words you uttered!
    Jupiter, how oft with your hand you wiped away the tears!

quis te mutavit tantus deus? an quod amantes
  non longe a caro corpore abesse volunt?
atque ibi me cunctis pro dulci conjuge divis
  non sine taurino sanguine pollicita's,
si reditum tetulisset. is haud in tempore longo   35
  captam Asiam Aegypti finibus addiderat.
quis ego pro factis caelesti reddita coetu
  pristina vota novo munere dissoluo.
invita, o regina, tuo de vertice cessi,
  invita: adjuro teque tuumque caput,   40
digna ferat quod siquis inaniter adjurarit:
  sed qui se ferro postulet esse parem?
ille quoque eversus mons est, quem maximum in oris
  progenies Thiae clara supervehitur,
cum Medi peperere novum mare, cumque juventus   45
  per medium classi barbara navit Athon.
quid facient crines, cum ferro talia cedant?
  Juppiter, ut Chalybon omne genus pereat,
et qui principio sub terra quaerere venas
  institit ac ferri stringere duritiem!   50
abjunctae paulo ante comae mea fata sorores
  lugebant, cum se Memnonis Aethiopis
unigena impellens nutantibus aera pinnis
  obtulit Arsinoes Locridos ales equus,
isque per aetherias me tollens avolat umbras   55
  et Veneris casto collocat in gremio.
ipsa suum Zephyritis eo famulum legarat,
  Graia Canopeis incola litoribus.
hic liquidi vario ne solum in lumine caeli
  ex Ariadnaeis aurea temporibus   60
fixa corona foret, sed nos quoque fulgeremus
  devotae flavi verticis exuviae.
uvidulam a fluctu cedentem ad templa deum me
  sidus in antiquis diva novum posuit:
Virginis et saevi contingens namque Leonis   65
  lumina, Callisto juncta Lycaoniae,

What god had power to change you? Or can those in love
  not bear to be far away from the beloved's presence?
And thereupon to all the gods for your dear husband's sake
  you vowed me together with blood of bulls,
if he accomplished his return. He in no long time
  had added conquered Asia to the territories of Egypt.
For which success I, duly delivered to the heavenly host,
  discharge with novel offering an old-time vow.
Unwillingly, O queen, I left your crown,
  unwillingly, I swear by you and by your head
(by which should any idly swear, let him reap his deserts)
  —but who can claim to be a match for steel?
Even that mountain was razed, the greatest on earth
  over which Thia's bright descendant travels,
when the Persians created a new sea and the orient's youth
  sailed in their ships through the middle of Athos.
What will tresses do, when such as mountains yield to iron?
  Jupiter, may the whole race of the Chalybes perish,
and he who first began to look for metal
  underground and forge bars of hard iron.
My sister locks were bewailing my fate, severed just before
  from them, when appeared the brother of Ethiopian
Memnon, beating the air with flapping wings,
  the winged steed of Locrian Arsinoe;
raising me on high, off he flies through the darkness of
  the sky and places me in the chaste bosom of Venus.
On this errand had our Lady of Zephyrium, the Greek denizen
  of Canopic shores, despatched her own messenger.
Hereupon, so that not only the golden crown
  from Ariadne's brows be set among the shifting lights
of the clear heavens, but that I too might shine
  as the consecrated spoil of a golden head, me as I came
to the abode of the gods dripping from the waves
  did the goddess set as a new constellation among the old:
touching the stars of the Virgin and the fierce Lion,
  and close by Callisto, Lycaon's child,

vertor in occasum, tardum dux ante Booten,
    qui vix sero alto mergitur Oceano.
sed quamquam me nocte premunt vestigia divum,
    lux autem canae Tethyi restituit   70
(pace tua fari hic liceat, Rhamnusia virgo,
    namque ego non ullo vera timore tegam,
nec si me infestis discerpent sidera dictis,
    condita quin imi pectoris evoluam) :
non his tam laetor rebus, quam me afore semper,   75
    afore me a dominae vertice discrucior,
quicum ego, dum virgo quidem erat, muliebribus expers
    unguentis, una vilia multa bibi.
nunc vos, optato quas junxit lumina taeda,
    non prius unanimis corpora conjugibus   80
tradite nudantes rejecta veste papillas,
    quam jucunda mihi munera libet onyx,
vester onyx, casto colitis quae jura cubili.
    sed quae se impuro dedit adulterio.
illius ah mala dona levis bibat irrita pulvis :   85
    namque ego ab indignis praemia nulla peto.
sed magis, o nuptae, semper concordia vestras,
    semper amor sedes incolat assiduus.
tu vero, regina, tuens cum sidera divam
    placabis festis luminibus Venerem,   90
unguinis expertem ne siris esse tuam me,
    sed potius largis affice muneribus.
sidera corruerint! iterum ut coma regia fiam,
    proximus Hydrochoi fulguret Oarion!

I wheel to my setting, leading the way before tardy Bootes,
    who sinks late, and hardly then, in the deep Ocean.
But though at night the steps of gods press close upon me
    and though day restores me to hoary Tethys
(by your leave, Rhamnusian maid, here let me speak,
    for I shall not from any fear conceal the truth,
not even if the stars rend me with cruel reproof,
    as not to unfold the secrets in the depths of my heart):
I do not so much rejoice at this as grieve at being parted,
    at for ever being parted from the head of my mistress,
along with whom, while still she was unwed, not enjoying
    matrons' perfumes, I drank many frugal scents.
Now you, whom with its welcome light the marriage torch has
    united, do not first yield your bodies to your loving
spouses, baring your breasts with opened robe,
    before the perfume-jar offers me pleasing gifts, the jar
that belongs to you who observe the laws of chaste wedlock.
    But as for her who has given herself to foul adultery,
ah, let the light dust drink up and nullify her wicked
    presents: I seek no favours from the unworthy.
But rather, o ye brides, may ever harmony,
    may ever abiding love dwell in your homes.
And you, my queen, when, gazing at the stars, you
    propitiate the goddess Venus on festive days,
suffer me not, who belong to you, to go in want of perfume,
    but rather enrich me with plentiful gifts.
The stars go hang! Could I become a royal lock again,
    Orion would be welcome to shine next to Aquarius!

LXVII

O dulci jucunda viro, jucunda parenti,
   salve, teque bona Juppiter auctet ope,
janua, quam Balbo dicunt servisse benigne
   olim, cum sedes ipse senex tenuit,
quamque ferunt rursus nato servisse maligne,   5
   postquam's porrecto facta marita sene.
dic agedum nobis quare mutata feraris
   in dominum veterem deseruisse fidem.

'Non (ita Caecilio placeam, cui tradita nunc sum)
   culpa meast, quamquam dicitur esse mea,   10
nec peccatum a me quisquam pote dicere quicquam:
   verum istuc populi lingua quiete tegit,
qui, quacumque aliquid reperitur non bene factum,
   ad me omnes clamant: janua, culpa tuast.'

Non istuc satis est uno te dicere verbo,   15
   sed facere ut quivis sentiat et videat.

'Qui possum? nemo quaerit nec scire laborat.'

   Nos volumus: nobis dicere ne dubita.

Dialogue with a door

POET

Greetings, door, dear to loved husband, dear to father,
    and may Jupiter favour you with kindly blessing:
they say that you served old Balbus well in time past
    when he occupied the house; and they also say that
conversely you served his son scurvily, when the old
    man was laid to rest and you became a bridal door.
Come, tell me why rumour says you have changed
    and have renounced your old loyalty to your master.

DOOR

Begging Caecilius' pardon, to whom I now belong,
    it is not my fault, though it is said to be mine,
nor can anyone say that I have done anything wrong:
    but this is a fact people's tongues keep quiet about,
who, whenever anything amiss comes to light,
    exclaim one and all 'Door, it's your fault!'

POET

It's not enough to say so with a flat denial,
    you must see that people know and acknowledge the fact.

DOOR

How can I? No one asks or cares to know.

POET

    I do: don't be afraid of telling me!

'Primum igitur, virgo quod fertur tradita nobis,
  falsumst. non illam vir prior attigerat,   20
languidior tenera cui pendens sicula beta
  numquam se mediam sustulit ad tunicam;
sed pater illusi nati violasse cubile
  dicitur et miseram conscelerasse domum,
sive quod impia mens caeco flagrabat amore,   25
  seu quod iners sterili semine natus erat,
ut quaerendum unde unde foret nervosius illud,
  quod posset zonam solvere virgineam.'

Egregium narras mira pietate parentem,
  qui ipse sui nati minxerit in gremium.   30

'Atqui non solum hoc dicit se cognitum habere
  Brixia Cycneae supposita speculae,
flavus quam molli praecurrit flumine Mella,
  Brixia Veronae mater amata meae,
sed de Postumio et Corneli narrat amore,   35
  cum quibus illa malum fecit adulterium.
dixerit hic aliquis: qui tu istaec, janua, nosti,
  cui numquam domini limine abesse licet
nec populum auscultare, sed hic suffixa tigillo
  tantum operire soles aut aperire domum?   40
saepe illam audivi furtiva voce loquentem
  solam cum ancillis haec sua flagitia,
nomine dicentem quos diximus, utpote quae mi
  speraret nec linguam esse nec auriculam.
praeterea addebat quendam, quem dicere nolo   45
  nomine, ne tollat rubra supercilia.
longus homost, magnas cui lites intulit olim
  falsum mendaci ventre puerperium.'

DOOR
Well, first, as to the girl's coming here a virgin,
    that is false. Her former husband had not touched her;
his dagger dangled more limply than an unripe beet
    and never rose to the middle of his tunic.
But the story goes that the father violated the bed of his
    dupe of a son, and disgraced the wretched family.
Perhaps his wicked mind lusted with ungovernable passion;
    perhaps the son was of sterile seed and impotent,
and from somewhere had to be found a stronger force
    to loose the maiden's girdle.

POET
This is a marvellously devoted father you speak of,
    to piddle in his own son's lap!

DOOR
But that's not all that is known to Brixia,
    Brixia, situated beneath the Cycnean citadel,
past which flows golden Mella with its gentle stream,
    Brixia, dear mother-city of my native Verona.
She tells of the intrigues of Postumius and Cornelius,
    with whom the lady committed base adultery.
Here someone will say 'Door, how can you know that,
    seeing that you cannot leave your master's threshold
or hear the talk of the town, but stuck here beneath
    the lintel can only open up or shut the house?'
Well, I've often heard her talking in hushed whispers
    alone with her maid about these escapades of hers,
mentioning the men I've named, as though
    she thought I hadn't got ears or tongue.
Moreover, she also spoke of somebody I shan't mention
    by name in case he raises his ginger eyebrows.
I mean the lanky fellow who once had to face a big lawsuit
    over an alleged confinement with its fictitious birth.

LXVIII A

Quod mihi fortuna casuque oppressus acerbo
   conscriptum hoc lacrimis mittis epistolium,
naufragum ut ejectum spumantibus aequoris undis
   sublevem et a mortis limine restituam,
quem neque sancta Venus molli requiescere somno   5
   desertum in lecto caelibe perpetitur,
nec veterum dulci scriptorum carmine Musae
   oblectant, cum mens anxia pervigilat:
id gratumst mihi, me quoniam tibi dicis amicum,
   muneraque et Musarum hinc petis et Veneris.   10
sed tibi ne mea sint ignota incommoda, Manli,
   neu me odisse putes hospitis officium,
accipe, quis merser fortunae fluctibus ipse,
   ne amplius a misero dona beata petas.
tempore quo primum vestis mihi tradita purast,   15
   jucundum cum aetas florida ver ageret,
multa satis lusi: non est dea nescia nostri,
   quae dulcem curis miscet amaritiem:
sed totum hoc studium luctu fraterna mihi mors
   abstulit. o misero frater adempte mihi,   20
tu mea tu moriens fregisti commoda, frater,
   tecum una totast nostra sepulta domus,
omnia tecum una perierunt gaudia nostra,
   quae tuus in vita dulcis alebat amor.
cujus ego interitu tota de mente fugavi   25
   haec studia atque omnes delicias animi.

A sorrowful reply to Manlius

That you, struck down by a bitter blow of chance,
    should send me this letter written with your tears,
a wrecked man cast up by the sea's foaming waves
    for me to help and rescue from death's door
(for holy Venus prevents you resting in gentle sleep
    as you lie deserted in a single bed
whom the Muses fail to charm with the sweet song of the
    ancient poets, since your troubled mind cannot rest),
this is gratifying to me, because you call me friend,
    and look to me for a gift of the Muses and of love.
But in case you are unaware of my own troubles, Manlius,
    or think that I shun the duty of a friend, let me tell you
of the waves of misfortune that engulf me, that you seek
    no more from a sufferer what only a happy man can give.
When first the white toga of manhood was conferred on me,
    when my youth's bloom was passing its happy spring,
I serenaded often enough: I am not unknown to the goddess
    who flavours her cares with a sweet bitterness:
but now grief at my brother's death has robbed me of all my
    enthusiasm for that. O brother, carried off to my sorrow,
you have in dying, yes, you brother, shattered my happiness,
    together with you all our house lies buried,
together with you all our joys have perished, those joys,
    which, while you lived, your dear love fostered.
Because of this loss I have completely banished from my mind
    all intellectual pursuits and pleasures.

quare, quod scribis Veronae turpe Catullo
  esse, quod hic quisquis de meliore nota
frigida deserto tepefactet membra cubili,
  id, Manli, non est turpe, magis miserumst.   30
ignosces igitur, si, quae mihi luctus ademit,
  haec tibi non tribuo munera, cum nequeo.
nam, quod scriptorum non magnast copia apud me,
  hoc fit, quod Romae vivimus: illa domus,
illa mihi sedes, illic mea carpitur aetas;   35
  huc una ex multis capsula me sequitur.
quod cum ita sit, nolim statuas nos mente maligna
  id facere aut animo non satis ingenuo,
quod tibi non hucusque petenti copia praestost:
  ultro ego deferrem, copia siqua foret.   40

So, as for your writing that it is a shame for Catullus to be
    at Verona, where everyone of the upper class has
to warm his cold limbs in an empty bed, it is on the
    contrary, Manlius, not a shame, it is rather a sorrow.
Pardon me then if I do not, because I cannot, present you
    with a gift which grief has snatched away.
As for my not having with me a large collection of writings,
    this is due to my living at Rome: there is my home,
there my abode, there is where I spend my life:
    only one box of many accompanies me here.
Under these circumstances I should not want you to think
    that I am acting unkindly or with an ungenerous spirit,
if you have not so far been supplied with your request:
    I should furnish you unasked, had I the supply.

LXVIII B

Non possum reticere, deae, qua me Allius in re
  juverit aut quantis foverit officiis,
ne fugiens saeclis obliviscentibus aetas
  illius hoc caeca nocte tegat studium:
sed dicam vobis, vos porro dicite multis   45
  milibus et facite haec charta loquatur anus,
versibus ut nostris etiam post funera vivat,
  notescatque magis mortuus atque magis,
nec tenuem texens sublimis aranea telam
  in deserto Alli nomine opus faciat.   50
nam, mihi quam dederit duplex Amathusia curam,
  scitis, et in quo me torruerit genere,
cum tantum arderem quantum Trinacria rupes
  lymphaque in Oetaeis Malia Thermopylis,
maesta neque assiduo tabescere lumina fletu   55
  cessarent tristique imbre madere genae.

qualis in aerii perlucens vertice montis
  rivus muscoso prosilit a lapide,
qui cum de prona praeceps est valle volutus,
  per medium densi transit iter populi,   60
dulce viatori lasso in sudore levamen,
  cum gravis exustos aestus hiulcat agros;
ac velut in nigro jactatis turbine nautis
  lenius aspirans aura secunda venit
jam prece Pollucis, jam Castoris implorata: 65
  tale fuit nobis Allius auxilium.

The unforgettable kindness of Allius

A : CATULLUS IN LOVE

Muses, I cannot bear to hide in what matter Allius
    helped me or cherished with what services,
lest the flight of time through ages of forgetfulness
    shroud in black night this kindness of his:
but I will tell you, and do you go on telling many
    thousands, and make this page speak in its old age,
so that he may live on in my verses even after death,
    indeed when dead grow more and more renowned,
and no spider weaving aloft her delicate web
    may ply her craft upon the neglected name of Allius.
For you know the suffering the treacherous goddess of love
    caused me and in what fashion she scorched me,
when I burnt as much as Sicily's volcano
    or the Malian spring at Thermopylae beneath Oeta
and my poor eyes never stopped melting with constant tears
    or my cheeks streaming with a sorry flood.

B : SIMILES

Like a crystal brook, which atop a high mountain
    gushes forth from a mossy rock
and after tumbling headlong down the steep valley
    passes straight across the highway thronged with people,
welcome refreshment to the traveller in his weary sweat,
    when the sultry heat causes the parched fields to crack;
and as to sailors tossed in a blinding storm
    comes the gentler breath of a favouring breeze
in answer to prayers now made to Castor and to Pollux:
    such a help did Allius prove to me.

is clausum lato patefecit limite campum,
   isque domum nobis isque dedit dominam,
ad quam communes exerceremus amores.
   quo mea se molli candida diva pede   70
intulit et trito fulgentem in limine plantam
   innixa arguta constituit solea,

conjugis ut quondam flagrans advenit amore
   Protesileam Laodamia domum
inceptam frustra, nondum cum sanguine sacro   75
   hostia caelestes pacificasset eros.
nil mihi tam valde placeat, Rhamnusia virgo,
   quod temere invitis suscipiatur eris.
quam jejuna pium desideret ara cruorem,
   doctast amisso Laodamia viro,   80
conjugis ante coacta novi dimittere collum,
   quam veniens una atque altera rursus hiems
noctibus in longis avidum saturasset amorem,
   posset ut abrupto vivere conjugio:
quod scibant Parcae non longo tempore abesse,   85
   si miles muros isset ad Iliacos.

nam tum Helenae raptu primores Argivorum
   coeperat ad sese Troja ciere viros,
Troja (nefas) commune sepulcrum Asiae Europaeque,
   Troja virum et virtutum omnium acerba cinis,   90

quaene etiam nostro letum miserabile fratri
   attulit. ei misero frater adempte mihi,
ei misero fratri jucundum lumen ademptum,
   tecum una totast nostra sepulta domus,
omnia tecum una perierunt gaudia nostra,   95
   quae tuus in vita dulcis alebat amor.

He opened up a broad path in a fenced field,
   and gave me house and gave me housekeeper,
beneath whose roof we might enjoy the love we shared.
   Thereto with dainty steps my shining goddess came
and checking her bright foot upon the polished threshold
   stepped on it with a tap of her sandal,

C: LAODAMIA

as on a time ablaze with love for her husband came
   Laodamia to the house of Protesilaus,
a house begun in vain, before a victim's sacrificial
   blood had appeased the lords of heaven.
May nothing please me so mightily, Rhamnusian maid,
   as to be rashly ventured against heaven's will!
How badly the starved altar thirsts for pure blood
   Laodamia learnt when she lost her man,
forced to let go her new husband's neck
   before the coming of a first and then another winter had
in the long nights satisfied their hungry love to the point
   where she could bear to live with her marriage broken off:
and this the Fates knew was not far off
   if he should go to fight before the walls of Ilium.

D: TROY

For then because of the rape of Helen Troy began
   to rouse against itself the foremost men of Greece,
Troy (horror!), the grave that Asia shares with Europe,
   Troy, bitter tomb of men and manly deeds,

E: CATULLUS' BROTHER

which brought upon my brother, too, a wretched
   death. O brother, stolen from me to my misery,
O precious light whose passing leaves your brother in misery,
   together with you all our house lies buried,
together with you all our joys have perished, those joys,
   which, while you lived, your dear love fostered.

quem nunc tam longe non inter nota sepulcra
  nec prope cognatos compositum cineres,
sed Troja obscena, Troja infelice sepultum
  detinet extremo terra aliena solo.   100

ad quam tum properans fertur lecta undique pubes
  Graia penetrales deseruisse focos.
ne Paris abducta gavisus libera moecha
  otia pacato degeret in thalamo.

quo tibi tum casu, pulcherrima Laodamia,   105
  ereptumst vita dulcius atque anima
conjugium: tanto te absorbens vertice amoris
  aestus in abruptum detulerat barathrum,
quale ferunt Grai Pheneum prope Cyllenaeum
  siccare emulsa pingue palude solum,   110
quod quondam caesis montis fodisse medullis
  audit falsiparens Amphitryoniades,
tempore quo certa Stymphalia monstra sagitta
  perculit imperio deterioris eri,
pluribus ut caeli tereretur janua divis,   115
  Hebe nec longa virginitate foret.
sed tuus altus amor barathro fuit altior illo,
  qui tamen indomitam ferre jugum docuit.

nam nec tam carum confecto aetate parenti
  una caput seri nata nepotis alit,   120
qui, cum divitiis vix tandem inventus avitis
  nomen testatas intulit in tabulas,
impia derisi gentilis gaudia tollens
  suscitat a cano vulturium capiti:

Whom now so far away and not among familiar tombs
 nor laid to rest among the ashes of your kin
but buried in hateful Troy, ill-omened Troy,
 a foreign land holds in a distant soil.

D: TROY

Thither then, they say, hastened the picked youth
 of all Greece and left their hearths and houses,
that Paris might not enjoy his stolen paramour
 and spend undisturbed leisure in a chamber free from war.

C: LAODAMIA

By that mischance then, fairest Laodamia, your marriage
 that was dearer to you than life and soul was stolen
from you: in such an eddy had love's tide engulfed you
 and dragged you down into a sheer abyss,
such as the Greeks say near Cyllenaean Pheneus
 drains the marsh and dries the fertile soil,
which on a time the reputed son of Amphitryon is said
 to have dug out by excavating the mountain's heart
when with unerring shaft he laid low the monsters
 of Stymphalus at a lesser lord's command,
that heaven's doorway be trodden by an increase
 of the gods and Hebe not remain unwedded long.
But your deep love was deeper than that abyss and
 taught you, though untamed, to bear the marriage yoke.

B: SIMILES

For not so dear to a parent worn out with age is
 the late-born grandson which his only daughter nurses,
who, found for his grandfather's fortune only just in time
 to have his name inserted in the witnessed will,
ends the impious joy of the thwarted next-of-kin
 and drives the vulture from the hoary head;

nec tantum niveo gavisast ulla columbo   125
    compar, quae multo dicitur improbius
oscula mordenti semper decerpere rostro
    quam quae praecipue multivolast mulier:
sed tu horum magnos vicisti sola furores,
    ut semel es flavo conciliata viro.   130
aut nihil aut paulo cui tum concedere digna
    lux mea se nostrum contulit in gremium,
quam circumcursans hinc illinc saepe Cupido
    fulgebat crocina candidus in tunica.

quae tamen etsi uno non est contenta Catullo,   135
    rara verecundae furta feremus erae,
ne nimium simus stultorum more molesti:
    saepe etiam Juno, maxima caelicolum,
conjugis in culpa flagrantem contudit iram,
    noscens omnivoli plurima furta Jovis.   140
atqui nec divis homines componier aequumst,
    nec mala, quot Juno quantave, nos patimur.
tolle igitur questus, et forti mente, Catulle,
    ingratum tremuli tolle parentis opus.
nec tamen illa mihi dextra deducta paterna
    fragrantem Assyrio venit odore domum,
sed furtiva dedit muta munuscula nocte,   145
    ipsius ex ipso dempta viri gremio.
quare illud satis est, si nobis is datur unis,
    quem lapide illa diem candidiore notat.

nor ever did dove delight so much in her snowy
 mate, though 'tis said that the dove is always
snatching kisses with biting bill more shamelessly
 than the most wanton of women:
but you alone exceeded the strong passions of these,
 when once you were mated with your golden-haired groom.
Yielding to her in naught or in but little was then
 my sweetheart when she brought herself into my arms;
and oft about her, flitting hither, flitting thither,
 Cupid shone brightly in his saffron tunic.

A: CATULLUS IN LOVE

And though she is not content with Catullus alone,
 yet shall I put up with the rare lapses of my discreet
mistress, lest I be a nuisance like stupid men:
 even Juno, greatest of goddesses, has often beaten down
the anger that has flared up at her husband's guilt,
 when she learns the lapses of all-lustful Jove.
Yet it is not fit that men should be confused with gods
 nor do we suffer the number or extent of Juno's wrongs.
So cease your complaints and with a firm resolve, Catullus,
 cease this unpleasing fussiness of an aged parent.
Moreover, it was not on her father's arm that she came
 to a house scented with perfumes of the orient
but gave me stolen joys in the silence of the night,
 snatched from very embrace of very husband.
Wherefore this is enough, if to me alone is given
 the day she distinguishes with a brighter mark.

LXVIII C

Hoc tibi, quod potui, confectum carmine munus
    pro multis, Alli, redditur officiis,   150
ne vestrum scabra tangat robigine nomen
    haec atque illa dies atque alia atque alia.
huc addent divi quam plurima, quae Themis olim
    antiquis solitast munera ferre piis.
sitis felices et tu simul et tua vita,   155
    et domus ipsa, in qua lusimus, et domina,
et qui principio nobis te tradidit Afer,
    a quo sunt primo mi omnia nata bono,
et longe ante omnes, mihi quae me carior ipsost,
    lux mea, qua viva vivere dulce mihist.   160

A postscript to the foregoing

This present, Allius, made up of poetry (the best I could),
    is rendered you for your many kindnesses, so that
your family name may not be touched by corrosive rust
    on this day or the next or another or another.
Thereto the gods will add all those many boons with which
    Justice once used to reward devotion in a bygone age.
Blessed be you all: you and your true-love together;
    the very house we played in and housekeeper, too;
and he of Africa who first gave you to us,
    from which first blessing have all my blessings come; and,
far above all, she who is dearer to me than my very self,
    my shining star, whose living makes life happiness for me.

LXIX

Noli admirari quare tibi femina nulla,
    Rufe, velit tenerum supposuisse femur,
non si illam rarae labefactes munere vestis
    aut perluciduli deliciis lapidis.
laedit te quaedam mala fabula, qua tibi fertur   5
    valle sub alarum trux habitare caper.
hunc metuunt omnes; neque mirum: nam mala valdest
    bestia, nec quicum bella puella cubet.
quare aut crudelem nasorum interfice pestem,
    aut admirari desine cur fugiant.   10

LXX

Nulli se dicit mulier mea nubere malle
    quam mihi, non si se Juppiter ipse petat.
dicit: sed mulier cupido quod dicit amanti,
    in vento et rapida scribere oportet aqua.

LXXI

Siqua jure bono sacer alarum obstitit hircus,
    aut siqua merito tarda podagra secat,
aemulus iste tuus, qui vestrum exercet amorem,
    mirificest, Quinti, nactus utrumque malum.
nam quotiens futuit, totiens ulciscitur ambos: 5
    illam affligit odore, ipse perit podagra.

The trouble with Rufus

Wonder not, Rufus, why none of the opposite sex
    wishes to place her dainty thighs beneath you,
not even if you undermine her virtue with gifts of choice
    silk or the enticement of a pellucid gem.
You are being hurt by an ugly rumour which asserts
    that beneath your armpits dwells a ferocious goat.
This they all fear, and no wonder; for it's a right rank
    beast that no pretty girl will go to bed with.
So either get rid of this painful affront to the nostrils
    or cease to wonder why the ladies flee.

Lesbia free to marry

The woman I love says there is no one she would rather wed
    than me, not though Jupiter himself should apply.
So she says; but what a woman says to an eager lover
    should be written on the wind and running water.

Fit punishment for a rival

If ever with justice the vile smell of the armpits has hurt,
    or if ever the laming gout proved a merited scourge,
the rival who makes love to your joint mistress, Quintius,
    has combined both maladies to a marvel,
for every time he gets on the job he punishes them both:
    torturing her with the odour, dying himself of the gout.

LXXII

Dicebas quondam solum te nosse Catullum,
  Lesbia, nec prae me velle tenere Jovem.
dilexi tum te non tantum ut vulgus amicam,
  sed pater ut natos diligit et generos.
nunc te cognovi: quare etsi impensius uror,   5
  multo mi tamen es vilior et levior.
'qui potis est?' inquis. quod amantem injuria talis
  cogit amare magis, sed bene velle minus.

LXXIII

Desine de quoquam quicquam bene velle mereri
  aut aliquem fieri posse putare pium.
omnia sunt ingrata, nihil fecisse benignest,
  immo etiam taedet, taedet obestque magis;
ut mihi, quem nemo gravius nec acerbius urget,   5
  quam modo quae me unum atque unicum amicum habuit.

LXXIV

Gellius audierat patruum objurgare solere,
  siquis delicias diceret aut faceret.
hoc ne ipsi accideret, patrui perdepsuit ipsam
  uxorem et patruum reddidit Harpocraten.
quod voluit fecit: nam, quamvis irrumet ipsum   5
  nunc patruum, verbum non faciet patruus.

LXXV

Huc est mens deducta tua mea, Lesbia, culpa,
  atque ita se officio perdidit ipsa suo,
ut jam nec bene velle queat tibi, si optima fias,
  nec desistere amare, omnia si facias.

Love changed to passion

You once said, Lesbia, that you belonged to Catullus alone
    and wished not to possess even Jove in preference to me.
I cherished you then, not just as an ordinary man a mistress,
    but as a father cherishes his children and their spouses.
Now I know you: so, though I burn more ardently,
    you are much cheaper and slighter in my eyes.
'How so?' you ask. Because such hurt as you have inflicted
    forces a lover to love more, but to like less.

The ingratitude of his dearest

Cease wishing to deserve any thanks from anyone
    or thinking that someone can ever become grateful.
Nothing gets any return; doing a kindness is no good: on the
    contrary it is exhausting, exhausting and harmful rather,
as for me, whom none oppresses more harshly or cruelly
    than she who but now had in me her one and only friend.

Gellius' uncle

Gellius had heard that his uncle used to lecture anyone
    who spoke of or indulged in sex.
Lest this happen to himself, he seduced his uncle's own
    wife and turned his uncle into the god of silence.
He has gained his object: for, even if he now stuffs
    uncle himself, uncle won't utter a word.

Devaluation of love

To this pass has my mind been brought by your perfidy,
    Lesbia, and so ruined itself by its devotion, that
now it can neither like you, though you become faultless,
    nor cease to love you, though you stop at nothing.

LXXVI

Siqua recordanti benefacta priora voluptas
    est homini, cum se cogitat esse pium,
nec sanctam violasse fidem, nec foedere in ullo
    divum ad fallendos numine abusum homines,
multa parata manent in longa aetate, Catulle,   5
    ex hoc ingrato gaudia amore tibi.
nam quaecumque homines bene cuiquam aut dicere possunt
    aut facere, haec a te dictaque factaque sunt.
omnia quae ingratae perierunt credita menti.
    quare cur tete jam amplius excrucies?   10
quin tu animum offirmas atque istinc te ipse reducis
    et dis invitis desinis esse miser?
difficilest longum subito deponere amorem,
    difficilest, verum hoc qua libet efficias:
una salus haec est, hoc est tibi pervincendum,   15
    hoc facias, sive id non pote sive pote.
o di, si vestrumst misereri, aut si quibus umquam
    extremam jam ipsa in morte tulistis opem,
me miserum aspicite et, si vitam puriter egi,
    eripite hanc pestem perniciemque mihi,   20
quae mihi surrepens imos ut torpor in artus
    expulit ex omni pectore laetitias.
non jam illud quaero, contra me ut diligat illa,
    aut, quod non potis est, esse pudica velit:
ipse valere opto et taetrum hunc deponere morbum.   25
    o di, reddite mi hoc pro pietate mea!

De profundis

If, remembering his former kindnesses, a man can feel
    pleasure, when he reflects that he has done his duty,
that he has not broken sacred faith or in any agreement has
    abused the sanction of the gods in order to deceive men,
then many joys in a long life await you, Catullus,
    earned from this ill-requited love.
For whatever good things men can say or do to any single
    person, these have been said and done by you.
All which has been thrown away on an ungrateful heart.
    Why then should you torture yourself any more? Why not
toughen your spirit and rescue yourself from your plight,
    and stop being miserable in defiance of the gods?
It is hard to cast aside suddenly a long-held love;
    it is hard, but somehow you must do it:
this is your only chance, this is a fight you must win,
    this you must achieve, whether possible or not.
Ye gods, if it is in you to have mercy, or if ever to any
    you have given aid at the last in the very hour of death,
look on me in my misery and, if I have led a pure life,
    rid me of this plague and pestilence, which,
creeping like a paralysis into the depths of my being,
    has banished happiness from every corner of my heart.
I do not now seek this, that she should love me in return,
    or, what is not possible, that she wish to be chaste:
I yearn to be well and to get rid of this foul disease.
    Ye gods, grant me this as a reward for my devotion.

LXXVII

Rufe mihi frustra ac nequiquam credite amice
   (frustra? immo magno cum pretio atque malo),
sicine surrepsti mi, atque intestina perurens
   ei misero eripuisti omnia nostra bona?
eripuisti, eheu nostrae crudele venenum   5
   vitae, eheu nostrae pestis amicitiae!

LXXVIII

Gallus habet fratres, quorumst lepidissima conjunx
   alterius, lepidus filius alterius.
Gallus homost bellus: nam dulces jungit amores,
   cum puero ut bello bella puella cubet.
Gallus homost stultus, nec se videt esse maritum,   5
   qui patruus patrui monstret adulterium.

LXXVIII B

Lesbi, non quererer te foedis moribus esse,
   si turpes tantum pollueres socios:
sed nunc id doleo, quod purae pura puellae
   savia comminxit spurca saliva tua.
verum id non impune feres: nam te omnia saecla
   noscent et, qui sis, fama loquetur anus.

The treachery of Rufus

Rufus, I thought you my friend, but in vain and for naught.
  For naught? Oh no, it cost me dear and brought me pain.
So this is how you've wormed your way into me, burnt out
  my guts, and robbed me, poor wretch, of all my blessings?
Yes, robbed, ah you vicious poison of my life,
  ah you blight upon my friendship!

The folly of Gallus

Gallus has two brothers, of whom one has a charming wife,
  the other a charming son.
Gallus is a pretty fellow, for he contrives a happy union
  by bedding the pretty girl with the pretty boy.
Gallus is a foolish fellow, and forgets he too is married,
  when teaching his nephew to seduce an uncle's wife.

An attack on Lesbius

Lesbius, I should not complain of your foul morals
  if you only corrupted your base associates:
but, as it is, I'm annoyed that your slimy spittle has
  sullied the pure lips of a pure girl.
But you won't get away with it: for all generations shall
  know you, and Fame in her old age will tell what you are.

LXXIX

Lesbius est pulcher. quid ni? quem Lesbia malit
  quam te cum tota gente, Catulle, tua.
sed tamen hic pulcher vendat cum gente Catullum,
  si tria notorum savia reppererit.

LXXX

quid dicam, Gelli, quare rosea ista labella
  hiberna fiant candidiora nive,
mane domo cum exis et cum te octava quiete
  e molli longo suscitat hora die?
nescioquid certest: an vere fama susurrat   5
  grandia te medii tenta vorare viri?
sic certest clamant Victoris rupta miselli
  ilia, et emulso barba notata sero.

LXXXI

Nemone in tanto potuit populo esse, Juventi,
  bellus homo, quem tu diligere inciperes,
praeterquam iste tuus moribunda ab sede Pisauri
  hospes inaurata pallidior statua,
qui tibi nunc cordist; quem tu praeponere nobis   5
  audes, et nescis quod facinus facias?

The incest of Lesbius

Lesbius is nothing if not handsome, and Lesbia prefers him
    to you, Catullus, and all your kin. Even so, friend
handsome would sell Catullus and his kin, if he could find
    three acquaintances willing to greet him with a kiss.

Gellius' secret

What shall I say to explain, Gellius, how your rosy lips
    become whiter than winter's snow
when you leave home in the morning and when the eighth hour
    rouses you from the relaxed siesta during the long day?
Something surely is afoot: it is true what rumour whispers,
    that you swallow the large tautness at a male's middle?
Yes, that's surely it: the ruptured loins of poor Victor
    cry it aloud, and your beard stained with milked sperm.

Juventius' crime

Juventius, could there not be found in so large a populace
    some nice fellow for you to start liking
other than that visitor you have from Pisaurum's rundown
    seat, the man paler than a gilded statue
who now holds your heart, whom you dare to prefer
    to me, and know not what a crime you commit?

LXXXII

Quinti, si tibi vis oculos debere Catullum
    aut aliud si quid carius est oculis,
eripere ei noli, multo quod carius illi
    est oculis seu quid carius est oculis.

LXXXIII

Lesbia mi praesente viro male plurima dicit:
    haec illi fatuo maxima laetitiast.
mule, nihil sentis? si nostri oblita taceret,
    sana esset: nunc quod gannit et obloquitur,
non solum meminit, sed, quae multo acrior est res,   5
    iratast. hoc est, uritur et loquitur.

LXXXIV

Chommoda dicebat, si quando commoda vellet
    dicere, et insidias Arrius hinsidias,
et tum mirifice sperabat se esse locutum,
    cum quantum poterat dixerat hinsidias.
credo, sic mater, sic semper avunculus ejus,   5
    sic maternus avus dixerat atque avia.
hoc misso in Syriam requierant omnibus aures:
    audibant eadem haec leniter et leviter,
nec sibi postilla metuebant talia verba,
    cum subito affertur nuntius horribilis,   10
Ionios fluctus, postquam illuc Arrius isset,
    jam non Ionios esse, sed Hionios.

Appeal to a rival

Quintius, if you would have Catullus owe to you his eyes
    or something more precious than eyes,
do not rob him of what is more precious to him
    than his eyes or something more precious than eyes.

The blindness of Lesbia's husband

Lesbia curses me roundly in front of her husband:
    this gives the idiot the greatest pleasure.
Fool, don't you realise? If ignoring me she said nothing,
    she would be cured: as it is, her reviling me proves
not only that I am in her mind, but, much more to the point,
    that she is angry. That is, is aflame and so must speak.

A Roman cockney

'Hadvantages' was what Arry used to say whenever he meant
    'advantages,' and for 'ambush' he would say 'hambush.'
And he was convinced that he had spoken splendidly
    when he had said 'hambush' for all he was worth.
So I believe his mother always spoke, so her brother,
    and so her father and so her mother.
When he was despatched to Syria everyone's ears had a rest:
    they heard the same words pronounced smoothly and lightly,
and thereafter had no dread of such pronunciation
    until suddenly there comes the hair-raising news
that the Ionian sea, on Arry's arrival there,
    is no longer 'Ionian,' but 'Hionian.'

LXXXV

Odi et amo. quare id faciam, fortasse requiris.
   nescio, sed fieri sentio et excrucior.

LXXXVI

Quintia formosast multis; mihi candida, longa,
   rectast. haec ego sic singula confiteor;
totum illud 'formosa' nego: nam nulla venustas,
   nulla in tam magnost corpore mica salis.
Lesbia formosast, quae cum pulcherrima totast,   5
   tum omnibus una omnes surripuit Veneres.

LXXXVII

Nulla potest mulier tantum se dicere amatam
   vere, quantum a me Lesbia amata meast.
nulla fides ullo fuit umquam in foedere tanta,
   quanta in amore tuo ex parte reperta meast.

LXXXVIII

Quid facit is, Gelli, qui cum matre atque sorore
   prurit et abjectis pervigilat tunicis?
quid facit is, patruum qui non sinit esse maritum?
   ecquid scis quantum suscipiat sceleris?
suscipit, o Gelli, quantum non ultima Tethys   5
   nec genitor Nympharum abluit Oceanus:
nam nihil est quicquam sceleris, quo prodeat, ultra,
   non si demisso se ipse voret capite.

Love and hate

I hate and love. Perhaps you ask how I can do this?
  I know not, but I feel it so, and I am in agony.

A beauty contest

Quintia is beautiful for many; for me she is fair, tall,
  straight. Yes, I so far allow these several points;
but that she is beautiful as a whole I deny: for there is
  no charm, no spark of zest in all her body.
Lesbia is beautiful: not only is she ravishing from head to toe,
  but has stolen for herself alone all the charms of her sex.

Love and faithfulness

No woman can truly say that she has been loved
  as much as my Lesbia has been loved by me.
No faithfulness in any contract ever proved so great
  as that which was found on my side in my love for you.

Gellius' guilt

How vile, Gellius, is he who frolics with mother and
  sister, keeping all-night vigil with clothes removed?
How vile is he who won't let his uncle be a husband?
  Do you know how much guilt he incurs?
He incurs, Gellius, more than limitless Tethys can wash away
  or Oceanus, father of the Nymphs:
for there is no guilt beyond that for him to attain to,
  not even if he lowered his head and mouthed himself.

LXXXIX

Gellius est tenuis: quid ni? cui tam bona mater
   tamque valens vivat tamque venusta soror
tamque bonus patruus tamque omnia plena puellis
   cognatis, quare is desinat esse macer?
qui ut nihil attingat, nisi quod fas tangere non est,   5
   quantumvis quare sit macer invenies.

XC

Nascatur magus ex Gelli matrisque nefando
   conjugio et discat Persicum haruspicium:
nam magus ex matre et nato gignatur oportet,
   si verast Persarum impia religio,
gratus ut accepto veneretur carmine divos   5
   omentum in flamma pingue liquefaciens.

XCI

Non ideo, Gelli, sperabam te mihi fidum
   in misero hoc nostro, hoc perdito amore, fore,
quod te non nossem bene constantemve putarem
   aut posse a turpi mentem inhibere probro;
sed neque quod matrem nec germanam esse videbam   5
   hanc tibi, cujus me magnus edebat amor.
et quamvis tecum multo conjungerer usu,
   non satis id causae credideram esse tibi.
tu satis id duxti: tantum tibi gaudium in omni
   culpast, in quacumque est aliquid sceleris.   10

Gellius' thinness

Gellius is nothing if not thin. Seeing that he has a mother
    so kind and so hearty, and a sister so attractive,
and an uncle so kind, and the whole place so full of girls
    related to him, why should he cease being thin?
Though he touch only what is forbidden him to touch,
    you will find any number of reasons for him to be thin.

Gellius' child

Let a wizard be born from the abominable union of Gellius
    and his mother, and learn the Persian way of soothsaying:
for a wizard has to be born from mother and son,
    if the monstrous faith of the Persians is true, so that
with acceptable incantations he can offer pleasing worship
    to the gods, melting the fat caul in the altar fire.

Gellius' sheer wickedness

Gellius, I hoped you would prove a staunch friend to me
    in this unhappy, this disastrous love of mine,
not because I did not know you well or thought you reliable
    or able to restrain your mind from base villainy,
but because I perceived that she for whom fierce passion was
    consuming me was neither mother nor sister of yours.
And although I was connected with you by long familiarity,
    I did not believe this cause enough to tempt you.
Enough you thought it: such is the delight you take in any
    offence which has some portion of sheer wickedness

XCII

Lesbia mi dicit semper male nec tacet umquam
  de me: Lesbia me dispeream nisi amat.
quo signo? quia sunt totidem mea: deprecor illam
  assidue, verum dispeream nisi amo.

XCIII

Nil nimium studeo, Caesar, tibi velle placere,
  nec scire utrum sis albus an ater homo.

XCIV

Mentula moechatur. 'moechatur mentula?' certe.
  'hoc est quod dicunt: ipsa olera olla legit.'

XCV

Smyrna mei Cinnae, nonam post denique messem
  quam coeptast nonamque edita post hiemem,
milia cum interea quingenta Hatriensis in uno
  versiculorum anno putidus evomuit,
Smyrna cavas Satrachi penitus mittetur ad undas,   5
  Smyrnam cana diu saecula pervoluent:
at Volusi annales Paduam morientur ad ipsam
  et laxas scombris saepe dabunt tunicas.
parva mei mihi sint cordi monumenta sodalis:
  at populus tumido gaudeat Antimacho.   10

Proof of Lesbia's love

Lesbia is for ever criticizing me and never shuts up
    about me: I'm damned if she's not in love with me.
How do I know? Because I've the same symptoms: I curse her
    all the time, but I'm damned if I'm not in love with her.

A rebuff to Caesar

I am not particularly keen, Caesar, to find favour with you
    or to know whether you are a white man or a black.

Mockery of Mamurra

Cock fornicates. 'What, a fornicating cock?' Why, yes.
    'Well, as they say, the pot picks its own potherbs.'

Cinna's masterpiece

The Smyrna of my dear Cinna, finally published
    nine harvests and winters after it was begun,
while the Hatrian half a million verses in a single
    year has been belching forth, the disgusting fellow,
the Smyrna, I say, will reach Satrachus' deep waters,
    the Smyrna will long be read till time grows old;
but Volusius' Annals will die before crossing the Padua
    and many a time will furnish roomy coats for mackerel.
Dear to my heart be the slender monument of my friend;
    but let the vulgar rejoice in their bloated Antimachus.

XCVI

Si quicquam mutis gratum acceptumve sepulcris
    accidere a nostro, Calve, dolore potest,
quo desiderio veteres renovamus amores
    atque olim junctas flemus amicitias,
certe non tanto mors immatura dolorist   5
    Quintiliae, quantum gaudet amore tuo.

XCVII

Non (ita me di ament) quicquam referre putavi,
    utrumne os an culum olfacerem Aemilio.
nilo mundius hoc, nihiloque immundior ille,
    verum etiam culus mundior et melior:
nam sine dentibus est. os dentes sesquipedales,   5
    gingivas vero ploxeni habet veteris,
praeterea rictum qualem diffissus in aestu
    mejentis mulae cunnus habere solet.
hic futuit multas et se facit esse venustum,
    et non pistrino traditur atque asino?   10
quem siqua attingit, non illam posse putemus
    aegroti culum lingere carnificis?

XCVIII

In te, si in quemquam, dici pote, putide Vetti,
    id quod verbosis dicitur et fatuis.
ista cum lingua, si usus veniat tibi, possis
    culos et crepidas lingere carpatinas.
si nos omnino vis omnes perdere, Vetti,   5
    hiscas: omnino quod cupis efficies.

To Calvus on the death of Quintilia

If aught that is pleasing or acceptable can accrue
    to the silent grave from our sorrow, Calvus,
from that pain of longing wherewith we renew old loves
    and weep for friendships we contracted long ago,
surely Quintilia feels not so much sorrow at her untimely
    death as happiness at knowing that you loved her.

A foul playboy

I didn't—God help me!—think it made any difference
    whether I sniffed at Emil's mouth or his arse.
That's not cleaner than this, nor this dirtier than that;
    in fact, his arse is cleaner and better,
for it has no teeth. His mouth has teeth a foot and
    a half long, gums like a worn-out cart-frame,
and, to cap all, a gaping smile like the open slit
    of a pissing mule in summer.
He lays many girls and makes himself out a charmer, and yet
    is not handed over to the grinding-mill and its donkey?
Aren't we to think a girl who touches him capable
    of licking the arse of a hangman with dysentry?

To a stinker

To you, if to anyone, can be said, foul-mouthed Vettius,
    that which is said to windbags and idiots.
For with that tongue, if need arose, you could
    lick arses and rustics' clogs.
If you want to polish us all off completely, Vettius,
    open your mouth: you'll achieve your wish completely.

XCIX

Surripui tibi, dum ludis, mellite Juventi,
  saviolum dulci dulcius ambrosia.
verum id non impune tuli: namque amplius horam
  suffixum in summa me memini esse cruce,
dum tibi me purgo nec possum fletibus ullis   5
  tantillum vestrae demere saevitiae.
nam simul id factumst, multis diluta labella
  guttis abstersti mollibus articulis,
ne quicquam nostro contractum ex ore maneret,
  tamquam commictae spurca saliva lupae.   10
praeterea infesto miserum me tradere amori
  non cessasti omnique excruciare modo,
ut mi ex ambrosia mutatum jam foret illud
  saviolum tristi tristius elleboro.
quam quoniam poenam misero proponis amori,   15
  numquam jam posthac basia surripiam.

C

Caelius Aufillenum et Quintius Aufillenam
  flos Veronensum depereunt juvenum,
hic fratrem, ille sororem. hoc est, quod dicitur, illud
  fraternum vere dulce sodalicium.
cui faveam potius? Caeli, tibi: nam tua nobis   5
  perspectast igni tum unica amicitia,
cum vesana meas torreret flamma medullas.
  sis felix, Caeli, sis in amore potens.

A stolen kiss

I stole from you at play, honey-sweet Juventius,
    a teeny kiss sweeter than sweet ambrosia:
but not with impunity, since for more than an hour,
    I remember, I was impaled at the top of a cross,
trying to excuse myself to you and unable for all my tears
    to wash away the least little bit of your anger.
For the moment it was done, you washed your lips with plenty
    of water and wiped them clean with your dainty fingers,
in case any contagion from my mouth remained
    as though it were some filthy whore's foul spit.
Then you hastened to hand me over, poor wretch,
    to angry Love and torture me in every way,
so that from being ambrosia that teeny kiss
    became nastier than nasty gall.
If that's the penalty you set on my unhappy love,
    I shan't steal kisses from you any more.

Two Gentlemen of Verona

Caelius and Quintius, the pick of Verona's youth,
    are crazy for Aufillenus and Aufillena,
the former for the brother, the latter for the sister.
    A pretty example of the proverbial brotherhood of love!
Whom shall I back? You of course, Caelius, seeing that
    the test of fire revealed your priceless friendship
in the days when a furious passion scorched my soul.
    All success in your love, Caelius! And the best of luck!

CI

Multas per gentes et multa per aequora vectus
    advenio has miseras, frater, ad inferias,
ut te postremo donarem munere mortis
    et mutam nequiquam alloquerer cinerem,
quandoquidem fortuna mihi tete abstulit ipsum,   5
    heu miser indigne frater adempte mihi.
nunc tamen interea haec, prisco quae more parentum
    tradita sunt tristi munere ad inferias,
accipe fraterno multum manantia fletu,
    atque in perpetuum, frater, ave atque vale!   10

CII

Si quicquam tacito commissumst fido ab amico,
    cujus sit penitus nota fides animi,
me aeque esse invenies illorum jure sacratum,
    Corneli, et factum me esse putum Harpocraten.

CIII

Aut, sodes, mihi redde decem sestertia, Silo,
    deinde esto quamvis saevus et indomitus:
aut, si te nummi delectant, desine, quaeso,
    leno esse atque idem saevus et indomitus.

At his brother's grave

After travel over many a land and over many a sea
    I have come, brother, for these sad funeral rites,
to present you with death's last tribute
    and speak to your unanswering ashes, though speak in vain,
seeing that fate has robbed me of your living self,
    alas, poor brother, so cruelly stolen from me.
But now, naught else availing, take these gifts, which
    ancient custom prescribes, a forlorn tribute to the dead;
take them moistened with a brother's many tears,
    and for all time, brother, hail and farewell!

Catullus promises to keep a secret

If aught was ever confided by a trusting to a silent friend,
    whose sincerity of soul was thoroughly established,
you will find that I am no less bound by their code,
    Cornelius, and have turned into the very god of silence.

An ultimatum

Please, Silo, either give me back my ten grand
    and then turn as angry and violent as you like,
or, if you are happy with the money, kindly stop
    playing the pimp, and an angry and violent one at that.

CIV

Credis me potuisse meae maledicere vitae,
    ambobus mihi quae carior est oculis?
non potui, nec, si possem, tam perdite amarem:
    sed tua, mi Tappo, crimina nostra facis.

CV

Mentula conatur Pipleum scandere montem:
    Musae furcillis praecipitem eiciunt.

CVI

Cum puero bello praeconem qui videt, esse
    quid credat nisi se vendere discupere?

CVII

Si quicquam cupidoque optantique obtigit umquam
    insperanti, hoc est gratum animo proprie.
quare hoc est gratum nobisque est carius auro,
    quod te restituis, Lesbia, mi cupido,
restituis cupido atque insperanti, ipsa refers te   5
    nobis. o lucem candidiore nota!
quis me uno vivit felicior, aut magis hac res
    optandas vita dicere quis poterit?

A charge denied

Do you think that I could ever have cursed my sweetheart,
    who is dearer to me than my two eyes?
I couldn't, nor, if I could, would I love her so desperately:
    silly Tappo, the accusation you refer to me is your own.

Mamurra the poet

Cock makes a play to mount the slopes of poetry:
    the Muses with pitchforks throw him headlong off.

An obvious inference

When a man sees an auctioneer attending a pretty boy, what
    is he to make of it except a desire to sell oneself?

Reunion with the beloved

If aught was ever granted to anyone who desired and prayed
    and never hoped, that is truly welcome to the soul.
So is this welcome and dearer to me than gold,
    that you restore yourself, Lesbia, to me who desired,
restore to me who desired and never hoped, that you return
    yourself to me. O day distinguished with a brighter mark!
Who happier lives than I in all the world? Or who can tell
    of anything more desirable than the life that is mine?

CVIII

Si, Comini, populi arbitrio tua cana senectus
    spurcata impuris moribus intereat,
non equidem dubito quin primum inimica bonorum
    lingua exsecta avido sit data vulturio,
effossos oculos voret atro gutture corvus,   5
    intestina canes, cetera membra lupi.

CIX

Jucundum, mea vita, mihi proponis amorem
    hunc nostrum inter nos perpetuumque fore.
di magni, facite ut vere promittere possit,
    atque id sincere dicat et ex animo,
ut liceat nobis tota perducere vita   5
    aeternum hoc sanctae foedus amicitiae.

CX

Aufillena, bonae semper laudantur amicae:
    accipiunt pretium, quae facere instituunt.
tu, quod promisti, mihi quod mentita inimica's,
    quod nec das et fers saepe, facis facinus.
aut facere ingenuaest, aut non promisse pudicae,   5
    Aufillena, fuit: sed data corripere
fraudando officiis plus quam meretricis avaraest,
    quae sese toto corpore prostituit.

Sentence by the people

If your hoary old age, Cominius, stained by an immoral life,
    were to end by the people's decree, I do not doubt that
first your tongue, the foe of the virtuous, would be cut
    out and given to the ravenous vulture, your eyes torn
out and swallowed down the raven's black throat,
    your guts devoured by dogs, the rest of you by wolves.

Catullus hopes and prays

You assure me, my darling, that this mutual love of ours
    will be happy and last for ever.
Ye gods, grant that she be capable of promising truly
    and say this sincerely and from the bottom of her heart,
so that we may our whole life long maintain
    this eternal compact of hallowed friendship.

The fraudulence of Aufillena

Kind mistresses, Aufillena, are ever praised:
    they receive payment for what they agree to do.
You, in cruelly cheating me of what you promised,
    in continually taking but not giving, are doing wrong.
To comply, Aufillena, were honest; not to have promised
    were chaste: but to snatch all that is offered and cheat
on the obligations exceeds the conduct of a grasping harlot
    who prostitutes herself with all her body.

CXI

Aufillena, viro contentam vivere solo
    nuptarum laus est laudibus ex nimiis:
sed cuivis quamvis potius succumbere par est
    quam matrem fratres ex patre concipere.

CXII

Multus homo's, Naso, neque tecum multus homost qui
    descendit: Naso, multus es et pathicus.

CXIII

Consule Pompeio primum duo, Cinna, solebant
    Mucillam: facto consule nunc iterum
manserunt duo, sed creverunt milia in unum
    singula. fecundum semen adulterio.

CXIV

Firmano saltu non falso Mentula dives
    fertur, qui tot res in se habet egregias,
aucupium omne genus, pisces, prata, arva ferasque.
    nequiquam: fructus sumptibus exsuperat.
quare concedo sit dives, dum omnia desint.
    saltum laudemus, dum modio ipse egeat.

5

The incest of Aufillena

Aufillena, to live content with one's husband alone is the
   greatest of compliments one can pay to wives: but it is
better for a woman to sleep with anyone at all than conceive
   by her own father and become the mother of brothers.

A punning taunt at a busybody

Naso, you're an active man, but not many men accompany
   you to the forum: yes, you're an active man—but a passive.

The growth of adultery

In Pompey's first consulship, Cinna, there were two to enjoy
   dear Mucia's favours: in his second term there are
still two at it, but each has grown to a thousand.
   Adultery has a fruitful seed.

An uneconomical estate

For his estate at Firmum Cock is rightly reckoned rich,
   since it has so many fine things in it:
fowl of every kind, fish, pasture, ploughland, and game.
   All to no purpose: his outlays exceed its returns.
So I don't mind his being rich, provided he's no assets;
   and let's admire his estate, provided he hasn't a bean.

CXV

Mentula habet juxta triginta jugera prati,
    quadraginta arvi: cetera sunt maria.
cur non divitiis Croesum superare potis sit,
    uno qui in saltu tot bona possideat,
prata, arva, ingentes silvas vastasque paludes   5
    usque ad Hyperboreos et mare ad Oceanum?
omnia magna haec sunt, tamen ipsest maximus ultro,
    non homo, sed vero mentula magna minax.

CXVI

Saepe tibi studioso animo verba ante requirens
    carmina uti possem vertere Battiadae,
qui te lenirem nobis, neu conarere
    tela infesta meum mittere in usque caput,
hunc video mihi nunc frustra sumptum esse laborem,   5
    Gelli, nec nostras hic valuisse preces.
contra nos tela ista tua evitabimus acta:
    at fixus nostris tu dabi' supplicium.

Explicit Catulli Veronensis Liber

No ordinary man

Cock has close on thirty acres of pasture,
    forty of ploughland: all the rest is swamp.
How can he fail to surpass Croesus with his riches,
    when in one estate he possesses so many good things,
pasture, ploughland, enormous woods and vast lakes
    as far as the Hyperboreans and the sea of Ocean?
All this is great, but the greatest of all is the owner,
    no ordinary man, but in fact a mighty menacing cock.

Gellius' implacability

Oft in the past with earnest thought I've searched for words
    wherewith to translate for you poems of the Battiad,
that I might win you over, and that you might not try
    to land deadly shafts upon my head.
But now I see that this has been toil vainly undertaken,
    Gellius, and that herein my prayers have not availed.
Those shafts of yours launched against me I shall evade;
    but you shall be pierced by mine and pay the penalty.

Here ends the Book of Catullus of Verona

SAPPHO, fragment 31 (cf. LI)

That man seems to me the equal
of the gods, who sits face to face
with you and listens nearby to
    your sweet voice

and lovely laughter, an experience which   5
makes the heart in my breast flutter;
for the moment I look at you, then I can
    no longer speak,

but my tongue is paralysed, a subtle
flame has at once coursed beneath my skin,   10
with my eyes I see nothing, and my
    ears are buzzing;

sweat pours down me, and trembling
seizes me all over, I am paler
than grass, and I seem to be on the   15
    verge of dying.

But all must be endured, since . . .

    (the rest of the stanza is lost)

CALLIMACHUS, fragment 110 (cf. LXVI)

Having surveyed the charted firmament, where move . . .   1

Conon saw me too on high, the lock of   7
    Berenice, which she dedicated to all the gods . . .

    token of the nocturnal struggle . . .   14

    I swore by your head and by your life . . .   40

    over which Thia's bright descendant travels,   44
the obelisk of your mother Arsinoe, and the Persians'   45
    destructive ships sailed through the middle of Athos.
What can we tresses do, when such as mountains yield
    to iron? May the race of the Chalybes perish,
who first brought it to light, an evil plant rising
    from the earth, and taught the work of the hammer.   50
Me severed just before my sister locks were bewailing,
    when forthwith the brother of Ethiopian Memnon,
the gentle breeze, eagerly fluttered his fleet wings,
    the steed of Locrian Arsinoe of the violet girdle,
seized me with his breath and carrying me through the   55
    humid air placed me . . . in the bosom of Cypris.
On that errand had he been despatched by Aphrodite of
    Zephyrion, denizen of Canopic shores.
And that not only the golden crown of the Minoan
    bride might shine upon mankind,   60
but that I too be numbered among the myriad lights,
    I the fair tress of Berenice,
me as I rose to heaven dripping from the waves
    did Cypris set as a new constellation among the old . . . 64

First proceeding in autumn to the Ocean . . .   67

These honours bring me not so much joy as grief   75
    that I shall no longer touch that head,
from which, while still she was unwed, I drank many
    frugal scents but did not enjoy matrons' perfumes . . . 78

Critical Notes

HERE are given details of all significant departures from the manuscript tradition when they have not already become the textus receptus (which I define as the reading common to the standard editions: Kroll, Merrill, Mynors, and Quinn). Thus at LXIV 344 *campi*, where actually the manuscripts read *teuen*, no note is given: the correction was made in the fifteenth century (on the basis of an imitation by Statius) and appears in all the standard editions. However, I also give a note where (as at I 2) this edition follows the tradition and the standard editions (or one or more of them) abandon it.

The matter of orthography warrants special mention. This edition conforms to the conventions of the early empire, which subsequently became the standard way of spelling Latin. But no standard had evolved by Catullus' day, and his manuscripts reveal clear traces of older republican spellings (e.g. *tuos* for *tuus*, *marei* for *mari*, *guro* for *gyro*). But these are the rare traces of a spelling system now virtually obliterated in the manuscript tradition. No editor has attempted to restore Catullus' practice. Indeed, to do so completely would be impossible, for there is no means of telling whether he wrote, for example, *inmemor* or *immemor* (both forms being in use in 55 B.C.) or even whether he was consistent with himself. Therefore, except where metre prescribes an archaic form (e.g. LXVI 28 *alis* for *alius*), a standard and uniform spelling has been rigorously enforced. Similar reasoning has encouraged the employment of *j* and *v*: *io* and *jo*, *soluit* and *solvit* were pronounced differently, and in LXI and II Catullus illustrates the difference.

The notes follow the conventions of an apparatus criticus, except that I have abbreviated scholars' names and dated all conjectures (a key is set out below). To avoid introducing irrelevancies I have once or twice (e.g. at III 16) interpreted the archetype's reading where it has been superficially corrupted: these readings are denoted by (*V*). And for the same reason I have accommodated conjecturers' spellings to the system adopted in the text. The manuscripts (cf. Introduction, pages 10f) are represented as follows: *V* is the archetype (codex Veronensis: ? twelfth-century) as inferred from the consensus of *O* (codex Oxoniensis: *c*. 1370), *G* (codex Sangermanensis: 1375), and *R* (codex Romanus:

1375 +). Other abbreviations are: *add*(ed by), *Ann*(otations, the relevant place in the), *edd*. (editions), *lac*(una postulated by), *suppl*(emented by), and *transp*(osed by).

Finally and importantly, verses printed in the text in small type are not found in the manuscripts, nor do they imply that gaps of that size are left in the manuscripts: they are scholars' illustrative supplements of lacunas conjectured for metrical or other reasons.

Sources of conjectural emendations

Humanists

a	pre-1412
b	pre-1424
c	*c.* 1430
d	*c.* 1450
e	pre-1452
f	1457
g	pre-1460
h	1463
i	1465
j	1467
k	pre-1468
l	*c.* 1470

Editions

pc	ed. princeps 1472
pm	ed. Parmensis 1473
ro	ed. Romana 1475
al	ed. Aldina 1502

Scholars

Av	Avantius 1495
Av²	Avantius *c.* 1535
Ba	Baehrens 1874
Ba²	Baehrens 1876
Ba³	Baehrens 1885
Bc	Bickel 1950
Be	Bentley *c.* 1697
Bg	Bergk 1854
Bg²	Bergk 1861
Bi	Birt 1904

Bs	Busche 1894
Bu	Burman 1759
Ca	Calphurnius 1481
Co	Conington 1861
Cr	Cornelissen 1878
Cz	Czwalina 1867
Da	Dawes 1745
De	Delz 1977
Do	Dousa fil. 1592
Ek	Eldik 1764
El	Ellis 1867
Fa	Faernus 1566
Fd	Friedrich 1908
Fo	Fordyce 1973
Fr	Froehlich 1849
Fr²	Froehlich 1851
Ft	Fruter 1571
Gl	Gulielmius 1582
Go	Goold 1969
Go²	Goold 1973
Go³	Goold 1983
Gr	Gratwick 1979
Gu	A. Guarinus 1521
Gv	B. Guarinus 1485
Ha	Haupt 1837
Ha²	Haupt 1853
He	Heinsius pre-1681
Hf	Hoeufft 1815
Hl	Halbertsma 1885
Ho	Housman 1889
Hy	Heyse 1855
Hz	Hertzberg 1843
Kl	Klotz 1859
La	Lachmann 1829

La²	Lachmann pre-1851		*Rc*	Richards 1895
Le	Lee 1970		*Ri*	Riese 1884
Li	Lindsay 1919		*Rm*	Richmond 1912
Ma	Maehly 1871		*Rt*	Ritter 1828
Mc	Marcilius 1604		*Sa*	Santen 1788
Me	Meineke 1852		*Sb*	Schwabe 1866
Mk	Markland 1723		*Sc*	Scaliger 1577
Ml	Mueller 1870		*Si*	Sillig 1823
Mr	Muretus 1554		*Sk*	Skutsch 1962
Mu	Munro 1872		*Sk²*	Skutsch 1969
Mu²	Munro 1873		*Sk³*	Skutsch 1974
Mu³	Munro 1878		*Sk⁴*	Skutsch 1976
Ni	Nisbet 1978		*Sl*	Sabellicus 1495
Ow	Owen 1893		*Sp*	Spengel 1827
Pa	Palmer 1896		*Sr*	Schrader 1761
Pd	Palladius 1496		*Sr²*	Schrader 1776
Pe	Peerlkamp 1843		*St*	Statius 1566
Pg	Postgate 1889		*Th*	Thomas 1890
Ph	Parrhasius 1534		*Tm*	J. A. K. Thomson 1950
Pi	Pighi 1961		*Tu*	Turnebus 1564
Pl	Pleitner 1849		*Vi*	Victorius 1585
Pn	Pontanus 1503		*Vo*	Vossius 1684
Po	Politian 1526		*We*	Westphal 1865
Pr	Parthenius 1485		*Wi*	Wilamowitz 1924
Ps	Pastrengicus pre-1362		*Wk*	Wilkes 1904
Pt	Passerat 1608		*Wm*	Wiman 1963
Ra	Ramler 1793		*Wn*	Wilkinson 1977
Rb	Ribbeck 1862			

I

2 arido *V*: arida *Ps*
9 quidem *pc*: quod *V*:
quod o *k*
p. ut ergo *Bg*: patrona
uirgo *V*

II

7f *transp. Mu*
8 cum . . . -et *Gv*:
tum . . . -at *V*
7 sit *Mu*: et *V*
9 posse *Vo*: possem *V* (*see*
Ann.)

III

16 quod *Go*: o (*V*)

IV

8 Thracia *Tm*: -am *V*
24 nouissme *V*: novissimo *g*

VI

11 nil perstare *Sk⁴*: nam inista
pre- *V*

VIII

6 tum *R*: cum *OG*

X

8 ecquonam *St*: et quonam *V*
10 nunc *We*: nec *V*
25 mihi' *Sk*[4]: 'mihi *edd.*
32 paratis *St*: pararim *V*

XI

11 quoque *Wn*: -que *V*

XII

9 differtus *Pt*: dissertus *V*

XIV

16 Salse *G*: false *OR*

XV

2 pudenter *Ma*: pudentem *V*

XVII

3 axiclis *Ow*: axulis (*V*)
   recidivis *Ni*: rediuiuis *V*
21 merus *Pt*: meus *V*

XXI

7 struentem *Rb*: instr. *V*
11 a temet *Fr*[2]: me me *V*

XXII

5 palimpsesto (*V*):
  palimpseston *Mc*
6 novae *Ni*: noue *V*: novi *pm*
  bibli *Ni*: libri *V*
9 tum *g*: tu *V*
12 putamus *Fo*: Putemus *V*
13 scitius *Ml*: tristius *V*

XXIII

10 facta *V*: furta *Ha*[2]

XXIV

7 quid *O*: qui *GR*

XXV

5 dives arca rimulas *Sk*[3]: diua
  mulier aries *V*
11 conscribilent flagella *Tu*:
  flagella conscribilent *V*

XXIX

4 ante *St*: cum te *V*
5,9 hoc *Ba*[2]: haec *V*
20 eine *Ba*: hunc *V*
  optima *Ba*[2]: timet *V*
23 o piissimi *Ha*:
  opulentissime *V*

XXX

4 num *Sb*: nec *V*
5 cum *Mu*[3]: quae *V*

XXXI

12 sal. *Go*: sal. o *V*
13 gaudente *Bg*[2]: gaudete *V*
  vosque *d*: uos quoque *V*
  limpidae *Av*: lidiae *V*

XXXV

6 tuique *Ni*: meique *V*

XXXVI

10 ac *add. Go*[2]

XXXVII

11 mi *He*: me *V*

XXXVIII

2 et est *Si*: et *V*
6 tuos *Ba*³: meos *V*

XXXIX

9 te *add. Ma.*
11 pinguis *Li*: parcus *V*

XL

1 Raude *Fa*: rauide *V*

XLI

1 Anneiana *Sb*: a me an a *V*
8 aes *Fr*: et *V*

XLII

4 nostra *Av*²: uestra *V*
13 facit *Hl*: facis *V*
14 potest *c*: potes *V*
16f *transp. We*
16 quo *We*: quod *V*

XLIV

17 ulta *V*: ultu' *Mr*
21 fecit *Ba*²: legit *V*

XLVI

11 uarie *V*: variae *Av*

XLVII

2 munda Ri: mundi *V*

XLVIII

4 mi umquam *St*: numqu. *V*
5 Africis *Mk*: aridis *V*

L

2 tuis *Sb*: meis *V*

LI

8 *lac. j, suppl. Rt*
11 geminae *Sr*: gemina *V*

LIV

1 oppido *Mu*²: oppido est *V*
2 tri- *Mu*²: eri *V*
5 Fufidio *Bc*: sufficio *V*

LV

2 latebrae *Pd*: tenebrae *V*
3 in *before* campo *Si*: *before* minore *V*
4 sacellis *Kl*: libellis *V*
8 video *Pr*: uidi *V*
   serrenas *d*: serena *V*
9 aufertis *Go*²: auelte *V*
   usque *Mu*³: ipse *V*
11 en inquit quaedam *Go*²: quaedam inquit *V*
   sinum reducens *Av*: nudum reduc *V*
13a *lac. and suppl. We*
LVIII 6ff *tramsp. ro*
   7f *transp. Mr*
   12 junctos *marg. G*: uinctos *V*
LV 14 te in *V*: ten *Mr*
   17 num *g*: nunc *V*
   22 nostri *var. GR*: uestri *V*
   sis *V*: sim *k*

LVII

7 lecticulo *O*: lectulo *GR*
9 socii *Av*²: socii et *V*

LVIII

8 magnanimos *k*: -mi (*V*)

LIX

1 Rufulum *Av*: rufum *V*

LXI

16   iunia *V*: uinia *h*
25   nutriuntur honore *Ma*: nutriunt umore *V*
46   anxiis *Ha²*: amatis *V*
77   ades *Sr²*: adest *V*
78a **ff**   *lac. El, suppl. Pi*
82   fles *Go²*: flet *V*
94   uiden *k*: uiden ut *V*
107a **ff**   *lac. Gu, suppl. Wi*
126   juvet *Bs*: libet *V*
140   soli *i*: sola *V*
170   urit in *Go²*: uritur *V*
215   ut *Bg* facie *Bu*: et facile *V* omnibus/ . . . insciis *Da*: insciens/ . . . omnibus *V*

LXII

9   vincere *Gv*: uisere *TV*
32a **ff**   *lac. Av, suppl. Go³*
35   Eoos *Sr²*: eosdem (*T*)*V*
39   qui *add. Sp*
41a   *lac. and suppl. Sp*
54   marita *T*: marito *V*
58   (*refrain add. Mr*)
59   et *TV*: at *al*
63   patris est *Ph*: patris *T*: -i *V*

LXIII

4   animi *Pr*: amnis *V*: animis *La*
9   tuum *La²*: tubam *V*
    Cybeb- *Be* (likewise 20, 35, 84, 91) -e *Si*: cibeles *V*
15   secutae *Bg*: exsecutae *V*
16   pelagi *V*: pelage *Vi*
42   excitam *La*: -um *V* (*likewise* 45 ipse; 78 hunc; 80 qui; 88 tenerum; 89 ille: *see Ann.*)
43   quem *Be*: eum *V*
54   operta *Ml*: omnia *V*
60   gyminasiis *El*: gymnasiis (*V*)
63   puber *Sc*: mulier *V*

75   dominae *Rc*: geminas *V*
85   rabidum *Sb*: rapidum *V*
    animum 'Itali' *Ba²*: -o *V*

LXIV

11   prima *b*: primam *GR*: proram *O*
13   incanuit *al*: incanduit *V*
14   freti *Sr²*: feri *V*
16   haud ante *Go²*: atque *V*
23   genus *V*: gens *schol. Veron.*
23a   um salvete bonarum *add. Pe*
24   mero *Pa*: meo *V*
31   quis *Ml*: quae *V*
35   Cieros *Me*: siros *V* (*see Ann.*)
37   Pharsalum *Pn*: pharsaliam *V*
40f   *transp. Ra*
73   ex *add. Ba³*
    quo *q*: -que et *V*
75   tecta *Pr*: tempta *V*
89   progignunt *k*: pergignunt *V*
100   quam tum *Fa*: quanto *V*
109   -que habet *Ba³*: eius *V*
119   lamentata est *Co*: leta *V*
140   miseram *pc*: misere *V*
148   meminere *Cz*: metuere *V*
164   conqueror *e*: conquerar *V*
174   in creta *Gr*: intortum *V*
175   haec *O*: hic *GR*
184   colitur *Pa*: litus *V*
186   (e)st *add. Gu*
205   quo motu *Hy*: quom tunc *V*
215   longe *Hf*: longa *V*
216f   *transp. Ba²*
227   decet *La*: dicet *V*
237   fors *Do*: aetas *V*
243   infecti *Sl*: inflati *V*
253a   (*lac. Bg*)
254   cui Thyades *Sk*: quae tum alacres *V*
276   vestibulo *Sr*: uestibuli *V*
282   aperit *Ho*: perit *V*
287   Haemonisin *He*: minosim *V* crebris *La²*: doris *V*
320   vellentes *Ft*: pellentes *V*

334 tales umquam *g*: umquam tales *V*
359 densis *Ni*: caesis *V*
382 Peleo *Go²*: pelei *V*
387 residens *Ba*: reuisens *V*
395 Amarynthia *Ba*: ramunsia *V*
402 uti nuptae *Ma*: ut innuptae *V*
novellae *Ba²*: nouercae *V*
403 improba *Ni*: impia *V*
404 penates *d*: parentes *V*

LXV

1 defectum *O*: confectum *GR*
9 *lac. c, suppl. Pa*

LXVI

7 in *Vo* limine *He*: numine *V*
9 cunctis ... deorum *Ha*: multis dearum *V*
11 auctatus *Go³*: auctus *V*
15 an quod aventum *Mu³*: atque parentum *V*
17 juxta *Go³*: intra *V*
21 et *O*: at *GR*
28 quo *g*: quod *V*
fortius *Mr*: fortior *V*
30 tersti *Av*: tristi *V*
48 Chalybon *Po*: -um *V*
58 canopeis *l*: canopicis *V*
59 hic liqu. *Fd*: hi dii uen ibi *V*
lumine *a*: numine *V*
63 fluctu *V*: fletu *Pd*
74 imi *Ni*: ueri *V*
77 quidem erat mul. *Sk²*: quondam fuit omnibus *V*
78 vilia *Lo*: milia *V*
91 ne *Ba²* siris *La*: non uestris *V*
93 corruerint *La*: cur iterent *V*
iterum *Mk* ut *Hz*: utinam *V*

LXVII

5 nato *Fr*: uoto *V*

12 istuc *Hy*: istius *V*
lingua quiete tegit *Pa*: ianua qui te facit *V*
20 attigerat *g*: attigerit *V*
23 illusi *Ba*: illius *V*
27 quaerendum unde unde *St*: quaerendus unde *V*
32 Cycneae *Vo*: chinea *V*
supposita speculae *Pn*: suppositum specula *V*
37 qui *al*: quid *V*
44 speraret *Ca*: sperent *V*

LXVIII

These three poems (like many others) are run together in the manuscripts and hence in many editions too.

LXVIII A

11, 30 Manli *f*: mali *V*
27 Catullo *g*: catulle *V*
29 tepefactet *Bg*: tepefacit *V*
39 hucusque *Ni*: utriusque *V*
praesto *Fr*: posta *V*

LXVIII B

42 foverit *Cr*: iuuerit *V*
47 *lac. G, suppl. Ba³*
63 ac *Pd*: haec *O*: hic *GR*
101 lecta *add. Ek*
102 graia *Ml*: graeca *V*
118 tamen *Hy*: tuum *V*
139 contudit *Hz* iram *Sa*: cotidiana *V*
141ab *lac. Mc, suppl. Go²*
142 opus *Pq*: onus *V*
145 muta *Hy*: mira *V*
148 diem *pm*: dies *V*

LXVIII C

155 ipsa *add. g*
157 te trad. *Sc*: terram dedit *V*

Afer *Mu*³: aufert *V*
158 mi *add. Ha*²

LXIX

10 fugiant *g*: fugiunt *V*

LXXI

1 siqua *V*: si cui *Ca*
jure *Pd*: uiro *V*
sacer alar. *Ca*: sacratorum *V*
2 siqua *Mu*³: si quam *V*
4 Quinti *Go*²: a te *V*

LXXIII

3 est *add. pre*-1878
4 taedet² *add. Av*
6 quae *Bi* (*Sk*²): qui *V*
(*see Ann.*)

LXXVI

3 in ullo *k*: nullo *V*
10 tete *Ba*³: te *V*
11 animum *St*: animo *V*
te ipse *El*: teque *V*

LXXVIII B

6ab *lac. Bg, suppl. Go*²
(*see Ann.*)

LXXX

8 barba *Ho*: labra *V*

LXXXIII

6 loquitur *V*: coquitur *Do*

LXXXIV

5 semper *Ni*: liber *V*

LXXXVII

3 in *add. Pd*

XC

5 gratus *Ml*: gnatus *V*

XCI

3 non nos. *Av* cognossem *V*

XCV

3 Hatr. in *Ho*: hortensius *V*
4 *lac. f, suppl. Mu*³
9 sodalis *add. al*

XCVI

4 junctas *Ba*³ (*De*): missas *V*

XCVII

2 -ne *add. Av*²
3 immundior ille *La*: -ius -ud *V*
5 os *Fr*: hic *V*

XCVIII

1, 5 Vetti *St*: uicti *V*

XCIX

8 mollibus *Le*: omnibus *V*

C

6 perspecta *g*: perfecta *V*
igni tum *Pa*: igitur *V*

CII

3 me aeque *Vo*: meque *V*
putum *Sb*: puta *V*

CIV

4 tua ... crimina nostra *Wk*:
tu ... omnia monstra *V*
mi Tappo *Go³*:
cum Tappone *V*

CVI

1 videt, esse *Th*: videt
esse, *edd.*

CVII

1 -que *add. al*
3 -que est *Ha²*: quoque *V*
7f res/optandas *La*:
est/optandus *V*

CX

7 officiis *Bg*: efficit *V*

CXI

3 ex nimiis *Ba²*: eximiis *V*
4 patre concipere *Wm*:
patruo *V*

CXII

1 est qui *add. Sc*

CXIII

2 Mucillam (= Moec-) *Pl*:
mecilia *V*

CXIV

6 modio *Rm*: modo *V*

CXV

1 juxta *Sc*: instar *V*
5 vastasque paludes *Pl*:
saltusque paludesque *V*
(*see Ann.*)

CXVI

1 verba ante *Pa*: uenante *V*
2 vertere *Pa*: mittere *V*
7 acta *Ba³*: amicta *V*

Annotations

Prefatory epigram. These verses, found in *GR* and bearing the name of Benvenuto Campesani (died 1323), declare that after being exiled in a distant place (presumably a monastery north of the Alps) Catullus (that is the archetype of our manuscripts) returned to Verona through the agency of a fellow townsman. The name of this person is allusively given, and scholars dispute its identification. A possible candidate is Cangrande I della Scala (1291–1329), overlord of Verona 1311–23 and Benvenuto's patron: the third verse will then derive his name from the French *can(n)e* = reed; and the fourth may refer to a statue or other representation of Cangrande situated in sight of a Verona thoroughfare (so the attractive theory of Harry L. Levy, who, however, extends it to an implausible identification). Otto Skutsch notes that in medieval Latin *papyrus* may mean 'wick' (a poet's way of saying candle or lamp): thus we have a pun in the last line clarifying the reference to Matthew 5:15 (*BICS* 16 [1969] 148).

Title. *Catulli Veronensis Liber*, exhibited by the manuscripts, almost certainly does not go back to the original edition: the toponymic would be unusual (perhaps added in a Verona copy out of local pride), and we should expect the full name, Gaius Valerius Catullus. Inconsistency in introducing ancient quotations from the poet suggests that no distinctive title existed, as would indeed be the case with posthumous publication of his collected compositions. Terentianus Maurus (*GL*.6.411.2899) has been adduced in support of *Liber Catulli*.

I. The work of Catullus, as it has come down to us, falls into three parts: I–LX (851 verses) short lyrics, mostly in hendecasyllables; LXI–LXVIII (1138 verses) long compositions in various metres; and LXIX–CXVI (322 verses) epigrams in elegiac verse. Since no book of classical Latin verse known to us contained anything like 2311 verses, or such a diversity of genres, Catullus cannot have written the dedication poem to introduce the total *oeuvre*, but rather, presumably, a collection of his lyrics (though not, as will be noted below, II–LX *exactly* as we have them).

Cornelius Nepos, biographer of illustrious men (the *World History* here referred to is no longer extant), was a compatriot about ten years older than the poet and a keen admirer of him; and was probably responsible for the collection and publication after the poet's death of the *Liber* which we possess. Nepos was not a patron of Catullus in the sense that Maecenas was of Horace but he had made a complimentary reference to him in his history (cf. lines 3–7), enabling Catullus to assert, tongue in cheek, that the patronage of his friend the historian will ensure for his little book (the polish of the roll suggests the polish of its contents) the immortality it might not win on its own merits.

II–XXVI. This section of the poet's *oeuvre*, in which all the hendecasyllables are composed with a heavy base (the second syllable always long), contains two principal sequences: (1) a Lesbia-cycle, sketching the development of the affair from innocence (II, III) to passion (V, VII) to disillusionment (VIII, XI); and (2) a Furius–Aurelius cycle (XV, XVI, XXI; XXIII, XXIV, XXVI). We may confidently attribute this design to Catullus except for VIII and XI (significantly the only non-hendecasyllabic poems in these cycles); they anticipate too much too soon. Possibly he planned to publish a book consisting of non-hendecasyllabic poems, in which the downhill course of his love affair was to be the dominant theme: beginning with LI, ending with XI, and containing in between many of the epigrams and elegiac poems we meet later. Whether or no, he never lived to do so, and the non-elegiac pieces, found among his papers after his death, were fitted into our collection by its editor. Lighted by *basiabis* in the penultimate line of VIII, he placed that poem after VII, and the last farewell, with its romantic travelogue, after X, another travel poem.

II. A one-sentence poem ending with a simile, like LXV. The swift-footed girl is Atalanta: she promised to marry the suitor who surpassed her in speed, and in the footrace with Hippomenes stopped to pick up the golden apples which he threw in her path and so (not altogether to her distress) was beaten.

9. *posse:* most editors retain the manuscript reading *possem* and place an exclamation mark after *curas*, where they judge the poem to end; verses 11–13 they take to be the tail-end of a lyric otherwise lost.

III. 'Venuses and Cupids' (also XIII 12) is an expression peculiar to Catullus, embracing all the agencies and personifications of Charm and Desire; 'Orcus', the ruler of the underworld, stands here rather for the underworld itself.

IV. In a shrine of Castor and Pollux on the shore of his Sirmio property Catullus is showing visitors a votive offering, a model (perhaps made of boxwood from Mt Cytorus) of the yacht which brought him home from Bithynia; and this poem is thus an unusual type of dedicatory inscription. The yacht, whose smooth and swift motion over the waves is artfully implied in the pure iambic metre, is made the authority for its own story, though this is related on its behalf by the poet. The sound of the letter *s* is prominent throughout and variously suggests the rustling of foliage, the whistling of sea-breezes, and the splashing of waves. Among the anthology of pieces alleged to be Virgil's juvenilia is to be found (*Catalepton* 10) a witty parody of this poem.

    8. *Thracias*, the wind from the NNW.

    11. *Cytorus*, a mountain (and town) on the Paphlagonian coast about 200 miles from the Bosporus.

    13. *Amastris*, a port about 25 miles west of Cytorus.

    27. Castor and Pollux were protectors of seafarers (cf. LXVIII B 65).

V. Written at an early stage in Catullus' love affair with Lesbia, his pseudonym (LI) for Clodia.

VI. The name Flavius does not recur in the poems. The poet's proposal at the end is obviously the very last thing his friend desires.

VII. A variation on V (and perhaps transposed from the key of XLVIII): this time the poet stands beside the lover, whereas then they were one. Cyrene was the chief centre for the export of *laserpicium* or *silphium*, the extract of a plant which had widespread use in medicine and in cooking. The oracle of Jupiter Ammon was situated in the oasis of Siwa in the Libyan desert; Battus was founder of Cyrene and the vaunted ancestor of Callimachus (LXV 16; CXVI 2).

VIII. The unsuspecting Catullus is stunned by Lesbia's rejection of him: he knows he has lost her (1–11) but his emotions cannot accept the fact (12–19). Note the staccato effect of the uniformly end-stopped lines, and a slight blemish: the poet everywhere addresses the lover in the second person, but in line 5 is obliged to use *nobis*, as *tibi* would not scan.

    Macaulay could not read this poem without being moved to tears; Wheeler thought that Catullus had 'with imagination and with humor' adapted motifs from Greek literature to his own case. The young Harvard scholar Richard Thomas has now (1981) identified what may have been an important source for the poet, the soliloquy of Demeas in Menander's *Samia*, 325–56; not that this affects the pathos or sincerity of the poem: 'It is quite simply that a poem, if it is to endure, will be a work of art, not an emotional outburst . . . We may detect emotion behind it, and we may weep when we read it; if so, that will merely be additional testimony to the poem's artistry.'

IX. Possibly a native of Verona like Catullus, Veranius elsewhere appears only with Fabullus (XII; XXVIII; XLVII), who also went to Spain with him, and is not otherwise known to us, unless he be the augural writer cited by Verrius Flaccus.

X. Catullus has recently returned from Bithynia, where he was accompanied, it seems, by Gaius Helvius Cinna (line 30: see XCV: he later became a partisan of Caesar's, but in the confusion which followed the dictator's murder he was lynched by a mob which mistook him for the conspiratorial praetor Lucius Cornelius Cinna). Friend Varus is probably Quintilius Varus (see XXII), who was to become an intimate of Horace and Virgil. The praetor (13) is identified in XXVIII as Memmius. A temple of the goddess Serapis at Rome was destroyed by order of the senate in 58, but was soon rebuilt by the faithful (not in other respects, perhaps, a pious segment of the urban population).

XI. Designedly composed in the metre of his first poem to her (LI, which we are presumed to recognize—the sapphics would otherwise not be an appropriate medium for invective—and which it echoes in the word *identidem*, 19) and contemptuously entrusted to his gutter-friends Furius and Aurelius, whose acquaintance we are presumed to have made in the obscene sequence (see XIV B, XVI). The Hyrcani dwelt in the southern confines of the Caspian Sea, the Sacae (commonly spelt *Sagae* in Latin) over a wide area roughly centred on the modern Tashkent. By contrast with his other references to Caesar, the third stanza is most naturally taken as a compliment and may even attest the reconciliation reported by Suetonius, *Julius* 73. Mention of the Britons proves that the date of composition is some time later than the summer of 55. The long preamble contrives to build up suspense, intensifying the vicious lash of the fifth stanza, just as the brief simplicity of the sixth evinces a tenderness that is no less arresting.

XII. The younger brother is Gaius Asinius Pollio (aged sixteen in 60), later famous as an intimate of Caesar, friend of Virgil (*Eclogue* 4) and Horace (*Odes* 2.1), and as orator, historian, and tragedian.

Veranius and Fabullus served together in Spain in or about 60. Saetabis (the modern Jativa near Valencia) was renowned for its linen, and the theft of a Saetaban napkin is one of the charges levelled against Thallus in XXV. It is to be remembered that the Romans ate with their fingers (the use of knives and forks is relatively modern) and guests were expected to bring their own table-napkins with them.

XIII. We are to suppose that Fabullus, using the formula *cenabo apud te* given by Cicero (*De Oratore* 2.246), had invited himself to dinner with the poet: here is the latter's retort. 'My sweetheart' must be the Lesbia of happy days, which suggests an early date, much earlier at any rate than XI. This is the only occasion on which Fabullus makes an appearance unaccompanied by his *alter ego* Veranius (cf. XII, XXVIII, XLVII).

XIV A. The Saturnalia, the great and happy festival in honour of Saturn, the ancient Italic god of plenty, fell on December 17 (though its revelry often lasted for several days more): Christmas has taken over much of its form and spirit, including the custom of exchanging gifts. Gaius Licinius Macer Calvus (L, XCVI), a neoteric poet like Catullus (he wrote an epyllion, *Io*), was also an eminent orator, especially famous for his impassioned speeches against Vatinius (cf. LIII), a political tool of Caesar's. Sulla is a nickname for Cornelius Epicadus, grammarian and freedman of Sulla the dictator. Caesius and Aquinus are unidentified; Suffenus we meet again in XXII. In the last sentence 'feet' is a pun, signifying also metrical feet.

XIV B. Only the first three lines of this lyric survive, but they suffice to show that the complete poem (illustrative supplement by editor) announced a sequence of obscene compositions, which indeed we have in XV to XXVI.

XV. The first of a cycle of poems about a boy-friend Juventius (who came of a distinguished family though is otherwise unknown: see also XL, XLVIII, LXXXI, XCIX, and CVI) and some unpleasant associates. The last two verses allude to an ancient punishment of adultery.

XVI. Furius and Aurelius play Rosencrantz and Guildenstern to Catullus' Hamlet: Aurelius is not further known, but many believe his partner in crime to have been the neoteric poet Marcus Furius Bibaculus of Cremona, who was a little younger than Catullus and must have been known to him. The language of the first line is metaphorical abuse, but carries in the last our hero's threat to prove his virility upon them literally at both ends.

XVII. About an acquaintance who is dangerously neglecting his young wife. Catullus, evidently not unmoved by her charms, would like to see the town's rickety bridge collapse under him. A similar situation (conceivably even the same) has inspired the defamatory LXVII. The Colony is Verona, and the leap-frogging god Mars, whose dancing priests were called Salii or Jumpers. The forests of Liguria were a special source of ship timber.

XVIII–XX. The manuscripts (which of course do not number the poems) pass immediately from XVII to XXI without any indication that anything has here been lost. The traditional numeration is due to Muretus, who at this point in his edition (1554) gratuitously inserted three Priapean poems: 1) the fragment *hunc lucum tibi dedico . . .* quoted by Terentianus Maurus 2755 as an example of Priapean metre and ascribed by him to Catullus; 2) *hunc ego juvenes locum . . . Anth.Lat.*775 Riese; and 3) *ego haec ego arte fabricata rustica . . . Anth.Lat.*774 Riese. There is not the slightest probability that any of these pieces or any of the other fragments occasionally attributed by editors to Catullus is authentic.

XXI. The mock title given Aurelius means something like 'King of the Hungry'; see also XXIV and XLIX. The boy of verse 4 is clearly Juventius (XXIV).

XXII. Suffenus (elsewhere only XIV 19) may be a nickname for Alfenus Varus (cf. XXX), in which case Varus in line 1 will also be he, although the latter is generally identified with the Quintilius Varus of X.

    7. *umbilici* (bosses), the knobs (which might be painted) at the ends of the wooden stick round which the papyrus was rolled.

    22. *manticae*, a double knapsack worn over the shoulder, having one pocket in front, one behind; we see only the pocket in front, which contains the failings of others (from a fable of Aesop's).

XXIII. The poverty of Furius (cf. XVI) is further lampooned in XXIV and XXVI.

XXIV. Here first we are apprised of the name of Catullus' boy-friend, introduced to us in XV. The preceding poem shows that the 'fine fellow' is Furius. Midas, king of Phrygia, like Croesus (CXV), serves as a symbol of boundless wealth.

XXV. On the same theme as XII. The Greek name Thallus ('Sprig') is servile and probably signifies that the addressee is a freedman. 'Scribbled all over' in 11 suggests the lash of satiric verse.

XXVI. A pun on the meanings of *opponere*: 'to place against' and 'to mortgage'.

XXVII–L. In a striking number of the hendecasyllabic poems between these limits (exceptions are XXVIII, XXXIII, XLIII, XLVI, XLVIII) the poet has, contrary to his practice up to this point, permitted himself light-based verses (i.e. having the second—or even the first—syllable short). Possibly this stretch of Catullus' work represents the second half of his *lepidus novus libellus* (11), though this metrical argument cannot apply to poems composed in other metres.

XXVII. A lyric to introduce (at least in the *libellus* designated by 1 1) a sequence of poems of invective. At drinking parties an arbiter was chosen to decree the proportion in which wine and water were to be mixed, here a Roman matron, the wife according to some of Servius Sulpicius Rufus, the famous lawyer and correspondent of Cicero: she was not a woman untouched by scandal. In verse 4 the unusual elision of two long syllables in succession reflects Postumia's tipsiness.

7. *This man:* I. Thyone was another name of Bacchus' mother, Semele; hence Thyonian, a follower of Bacchus.

XXVIII. Veranius and Fabullus, who have made a second tour abroad, are back from service on the staff of Lucius Calpurnius Piso Caesoninus, Caesar's father-in-law and governor of Macedonia 57–55. Piso's magnificent Herculanean villa, filled with bronzes of Greek provenance and what seems to be Philodemus' library (see XLVII), was discovered in 1750 and has since been partially excavated. Catullus returned in 56 from his service in Bithynia under Gaius Memmius (X), the son-in-law of Sulla and the patron of Lucretius. The obscene language concluding the poem signifies merely that Piso had thwarted the hopes of Veranius and Fabullus to enrich themselves as Memmius had those of Catullus.

14. *vobis:* Piso and Memmius, of course.

XXIX. Mamurra, a knight from Formiae, was a special target of Catullus' detestation. As an outstanding staff engineer of first Pompey ('pansy Romulus') in Pontus (the Mithridatic War) in 66 and then Caesar ('general without peer') in Spain in 61 he made and squandered fortunes, and was sufficiently practised with women to be given the nickname Mentula (line 13: cf. CV, CXIV, CXV). Line 3 refers to Transalpine Gaul, where males wore the hair long. The son-in-law is Pompey, who married Caesar's daughter Julia. Mention of Britain dates the poem to 54. 'Honourable' (line 23): ironical.

XXX. Alfenus Varus, who from cobbling in Verona rose to eminence as a jurist in Rome, is thought by some to be the Suffenus of XIV A and XXII. His offence against Catullus is unknown. While it may be that the poem expresses 'the morbidly exaggerated utterances of a distempered mind in, perhaps, a sick body, fancying itself deserted by former friends' (Merrill), it is more likely that the awkwardnesses and obscurity of the poem reflect the difficulties Catullus encountered in handling the Greater Asclepiad, of which we have no other example from his pen.

XXXI. Several of Catullus' non-hendecasyllable lyrics sit uncomfortably in their surroundings. Can it really have been the poet who placed this jewel (or XXXIV) in the invective section announced in XXVII? It was written on his return from Bithynia in 56, no doubt in the summer villa the Catulli possessed at Sirmio, situated at the southern end of the Lago di Garda.

5. The Thyni, as distinct from the Bithyni, were a Thracian tribe, who anciently settled in the portion of Bithynia nearest the Bosporus; but Catullus uses the name in mock pomposity to express his relief at having quitted the province.

XXXII. 'Contents, execrable. Date, indeterminable. Metre, Phalaecean' (Merrill) (!).

XXXIII. The theft of clothing at the baths (Skutsch refers this to the man who after using them put on another man's clothes) was deplored by Roman authors from Plautus to Petronius and beyond. Outside this poem the Vibennii are unknown.

XXXIV. A choir of boys and girls is imagined as performing this poem. As a result of Greek influence the old Italian goddess Diana assimilated the functions and associations of Artemis, Hecate, and the Moon. See also Introduction, page 18, and note on XXXI.

15f.   *notho . . ./. . . lumine luna:* a borrowing from Lucretius 5.575, which dates the poem to 54.

XXXV.   Caecilius is possibly he of the same name mentioned in LXVII and possibly an ancestor of Pliny the Younger, who was a Caecilius and came from Novum Comum; this was a colony established by Caesar in 59 and situated at the southern end of the western arm of the Lago di Como (*Lacus Larius*). Some time earlier Caecilius had begun a poem 'The Great Mother' (probably an epyllion like LXIV) but since then there has not been the slightest sign of progress. He is now involved in a passionate love affair, and Catullus—with a humorous reference to the girl—deviously inquires what has become of the poem. The friend of the sixth verse is Catullus himself; Dindymus was a mountain in Phrygia, a centre of the worship of Cybele, the Great Mother (cf. LXIII 13).

XXXVI.   Lesbia has promised that, if Catullus returns to her, she will consign to the flames (the limping deity is Vulcan) selected compositions of the worst of poets, meaning scurrilous verses by Catullus; instead, he takes her to mean that she will burn the long-winded epic of Volusius (XCV). The place-names in 12–14 are cult-centres of Venus: Idalium, Amathus, and Golgi in Cyprus; Cnidus in Caria. Dyrrachium is the Illyrian port for Italy; and Urii and Ancon are stopping-places on the Italian Adriatic for ships travelling to the north (suggesting Catullus' route home from the east in 56).

XXXVII.   Though in his exaggerated abuse he refers to it as a tavern, Catullus is alluding to Clodia's fashionable house on the Palatine, a stone's throw from the Temple of Castor and Pollux, the brothers often represented as wearing an egg-shaped cap. He is no longer *persona grata* there and lashes out at those who are, especially the reigning favourite Egnatius (cf. XXXIX): this worthy, who came from Celtiberia (roughly the central part of north-eastern Spain), belonged to an anti-neoteric school and wrote a *De Rerum Natura*.

XXXVIII.   A playful poem, which line 3 shows we are not to take too seriously, addressed to Cornificius, another neoteric poet. Simonides of Ceos (flor. 500) excelled in lyric dirges, his most famous composition being the two-line epigram commemorating the Spartan fallen at Thermopylae.

XXXIX. Continuing the theme of the last poem but one (cf. v, vII; XLI, XLIII).

XL. The name Ravidus ('Darky') does not occur elsewhere, and may here be used as a disguise, possibly for Aurelius, who in xv provokes a similar outburst of jealousy in respect of Juventius.

XLI. The toponymic is unfortunately corrupt, but probably refers to Anneianum, a town 28 miles south-east of Verona, and certainly we must look for the girl's home-town in Cisalpine Gaul (cf. XLIII 6). The Formian bankrupt is Mamurra (XXIX).

XLII. Custom in ancient Italy sanctioned a form of popular justice taken outside the law against someone from whom restitution was sought. The complainant, with a band of his supporters, accosted the offending party in a public place and demanded what was owed him in a forthright, not to say abusive, manner. It is by this process that Catullus here charges 'all the hendecasyllables there are' (i.e. the verse of invective personified) to secure the return of his writing-tablets from a girl variously fancied to be Ipsitilla (XXXII), Aufillena (CX), and her of the preceding poem. And, since Catullus chooses not to identify her, perhaps she was someone else—though not Lesbia, whom even at her most degraded he does not treat as a common woman.

XLIII. See on XLII. The reference to Lesbia implies that Catullus is in favour, or hopes to be.

XLIV. An elaborate pun: Sestius' speech has given Catullus a cold because it is composed in the 'frigid' (i.e. bombastic) style of Asianic oratory. Publius Sestius was a minor politician defended by Cicero on a charge of violence in 56; the date of his speech against Antius, apparently for electioneering malpractices, is not known. A country place at Tibur (modern Tivoli) was much more fashionable than one in the Sabine uplands.

XLV. The poet's last joyful expression of romantic love. It is 55, and though the young men of Rome are flocking to enlist in the campaigns against Britain and Syria, Septimius (unknown) is oblivious of everything save his Acme (a Greek freedwoman). Catullus' idyllic picture of the couple captures their endearing innocence without being spoiled by cynicism. For the Greeks and the Romans a sneeze was a good omen, and 'we may assume that a sneeze both to the left and to the right was the very eye of benediction' (McDaniel).

XLVI. Spring, 56. Nicaea was the administrative capital of Bithynia. We get some idea of Catullus' route home from IV, which implies that he travelled southward along the Ionian coast as far as Rhodes.

XLVII. A pendant to XXVIII. The first favourite is probably Gaius Porcius Cato, the tribune of 56, and Socration (pseudo-Socrates) a nickname for the Epicurean philosopher Philodemus, to whom Piso (and not only he) was much attached. Philodemus was also a poet, some thirty of his compositions being preserved in the *Greek Anthology*, and was altogether a more considerable figure than one would surmise from the mention of him here. Priapus, the god of procreation, occasionally suffers the indignity of having his name applied to the lustful as a term of abuse.

6. *de die:* The working day at Rome ended about the ninth hour; to dine before that was deemed the height of luxury.

XLVIII. This lyric, in heavy-based hendecasyllables, was perhaps the model for V and VII, in which the theme is transposed to a different key.

XLIX. A saucy expression of thanks to Cicero for having paid some compliment to Catullus as a poet. The grandiose apostrophe, the formal style of the vocative, and the exaggerated portraits of the poet and the orator show that, as in I, Catullus is writing tongue in cheek. And there is a sting in the tail of the poem, where *optimus omnium patronus* can mean not only 'the best of all advocates, but also 'the best advocate-of-all', i.e. the greatest unprincipled advocate. Since Cicero after attacking the villainous Vatinius in 56 defended him two years later, he was certainly vulnerable to such a taunt, and some have understandably ascribed the poem to the latter occasion, when in spite of Calvus' eloquence (LIII) Vatinius was acquitted.

L. Licinius is Calvus (XIV), immortalized as Catullus' friend and fellow-poet in Ovid's elegy on Tibullus (*Amores* 3.9.62). The setting of the scene in verses 1–6, which Calvus did not require to be told, shows that Catullus composed the poem for a larger audience than its addressee.

LI–LX. The sequence of hendecasyllabic poems beginning with XXVII and characterized by light metrical bases ends with L, which Clausen sees as the finale of the *lepidus novus libellus*. The remaining compositions preceding the long poems will have been inserted here by the posthumous editor. It is easy to imagine reasons why Catullus left them out: incomplete sense (LX), imperfect artistry (LII, LV), excessive obscenity (LVI, LVIII, LIX), tasteless invective (LIV, LVII). LI (like XI) had been intended for another book (see on II–XXVI above) and was probably placed after L because of the purely verbal connection between LI 13 *otium* and L 1 *otiosi*. LIII seems unobjectionable, though *salaputium* (a designation of the male organ) may, if Calvus took offence at its application to him, have caused its exclusion.

LI.   This piece, which gave his sweetheart her lyric name and served as his first approach to her, was the earlier of Catullus' two Sapphic odes: it closely follows a composition by the Greek poetess, in the opening stanzas of which she describes the overwhelming effect upon her of the beauty of one of her pupils and in the last bids herself exercise self-control (for an English translation see page 194). It is natural to identify the man in Catullus' adaptation as Clodia's husband, Quintus Caecilius Metellus Celer (consul 60). That the poem should be placed so late in Catullus' collected works (especially later than XI, which was written as a repudiation of it) is misleading and inappropriate (see note above).

LII.   Written in 54, when Lucius Nonius Sufenas was curule aedile and Vatinius (cf. LIII), who had defeated Cato for the praetorship, was so confident of his election as consul that he acted as though he already were (without justification, however, for he only became consul suffectus, and that merely for a few days, in December, 47).

LIII.   Placed here to follow the mention of Vatinius in LII. This oration of Calvus (XIV) was delivered at the trial of Publius Vatinius for election malpractices in 54. 'Am I to be convicted,' said the defendant, 'just because that devil has an eloquent tongue?' Calvus was a man of exiguous stature. See also XLIX.

LIV.   All that one can safely say about this desperately corrupt poem (here given after Munro) is that it is a scurrilous attack on Caesar and, with its echo of XXIX 11, a late one, too. Lucius Scribonius Libo was the father-in-law of Sextus Pompeius, but the other names mentioned in the poem cannot be identified with any confidence.

LV.   Camerius, a mischievous boy, who is (remarkably for his respectable name) a boudoir pet of Lesbia's (LVI 5), has led Catullus a wild-goose chase all over Rome. This *jeu d'esprit*, an extraordinary alternation of regular and syncopated hendecasyllables, framing an allegro movement devoted to mythological speedsters, suggests the breath-taking nature of the search.

3ff.   Referred to are a recreation ground adjoining the larger Campus Martius; the Circus Maximus; the temple of Jupiter on the Capitoline hill; and the sumptuous portico attached to Pompey's theatre built on the Campus Martius in his second consulship (55).

LVIII 6.   *the fabled sentinel*, Talos, the bronze robot of Minos who strode round Crete three times a day destroying invaders.

8.   *Ladas*, of Sparta, a famous Olympic champion. *Perseus* borrowed winged sandals from the Nymphs for his fight against Medusa.

7.   *Pegasus*, the winged horse who sprang from the blood of Medusa as her head was severed by Perseus.

9.   *Rhesus*, king of Thrace, whose famous snow-white horses were stolen by Ulysses and Diomedes on the night of his arrival in Troy.

LVI.   A punning obscenity (*caedere*: 'to cane as punishment' and 'to pedicate') addressed to Valerius Cato, a fellow countryman of Catullus and a prominent neoteric. The *dramatis personae* number two, Catullus and Camerius of the previous poem, not three (a common misinterpretation).

LVII.   Besides his military memoirs Caesar wrote a grammatical treatise *De Analogia*, two speeches against Cato the Younger, and a poem called *Iter*. Mamurra's poetical activity is alluded to in cv.

LVIII.   Addressed to Marcus Caelius Rufus, brilliant and profligate, a slightly younger member of the same fast set as Catullus, whom he had supplanted in Lesbia's (Clodia's) affections only to be discarded in turn. Clodia had him prosecuted in 56 on a charge of attempted poisoning, but he was successfully defended by Cicero in a colourful speech (*Pro Caelio*) still extant. At first a supporter of the senatorial cause he later declared for Caesar, by whom in 48 he was appointed praetor; he died the same year in a fruitless insurrection. See also LXVIII C, LXIX, LXXVII, and C.

LIX.   As the plural verb in the third line reveals, this poisonous pasquinade was composed as for public display. In placing it after LVIII the editor may have imagined some connection between Rufa and

Caelius Rufus, but it is clearly the lady who is being got at. Menenius is unknown.

5. *ustore*, the undertaker's slave, whose half-tonsure brands him as a runaway.

LX. A fragment found among the poet's papers. This *cri de coeur*, which echoes Ariadne's words in LXIV 115ff, is perhaps aimed at Lesbia. Remarkably, the first and last letters of each line may be read as an acrostic *natu ceu aes* 'by nature as unfeeling as bronze'.

LXI–LXIV. Baehrens labels these poems *Liber Secundus*, though there is no evidence that Catullus' poems were ever divided into books; indeed, since the ancients who cite Catullus never give a book-number and are clearly embarrassed about a reference ('*in Epithalamio*' says Quintilian—for example—quoting from LXII), we must infer that the whole corpus was from the beginning issued as a single book (*Catulli Veronensis Liber*). In spite of the fact that LXI–LXIV total 810 lines, a suitable amount for a book-roll, the editor's design is otherwise: he made LXIV the centre-piece of the whole collection and flanked it with long lyric and long elegiac, this section of long poems flanked in turn by the *libellus* (short lyric) and the epigrams (short elegiac).

LXI. Though the lyric form of this exquisite marriage-song is Greek, the spirit it breathes and the wedding it celebrates are wholly Roman. By careful artistry Catullus (who is the speaker throughout) contrives to suggest the sequence of the ceremony: first, Hymen, the wedding god, is invoked and the bride and the bridesmaids prepared; then the poet exhorts the bride to come forth; at the mid-point of the poem we are to imagine ourselves transported ahead to the bridegroom's house, from which we see the approach of the procession (symmetry suggests that a stanza has been lost) and follow it to the ritual placing of the bride upon the couch; the last section formally summons the groom and blesses the marriage of the couple. He, Lucius Manlius Torquatus (see LXVIII), born about 89, attracted the admiration of Cicero, who makes him a speaker in the *De Finibus* and eulogizes him in the *Brutus*; he became praetor in 49, and in the civil war espoused and in 46 died for the senatorial cause. His bride, who came of a plebeian family, had been adopted into the house of the Junii; Lucius Aurunculeius Cotta, the legate of Caesar's who perished in Gaul in 54, was conceivably her brother.

2. *Urania*, here as in Callimachus (frag. 2a) Hymen's mother, though usually the Muse of astronomy.

17. *Idalium*, a cult-centre of Venus in Cyprus.

18. *the Phrygian judge*, Paris, who awarded to Venus the apple of Discord ('For the most beautiful').

27. *Thespiae*, a village at the foot of Mount Helicon on the Boeotian (= Aonian) side.

120. *Fescennine jesting*, ribald verses traditionally sung at weddings; the name derives from the Faliscan town of Fescennium.

127. *Talassius*, a Roman marriage-god, the counterpart of the Greek Hymen.

173. Ellis posited here the loss of a stanza describing the bride's approach to the marriage-chamber.

175. The bride was usually escorted by three boys, one to precede with a torch, and one on either side to support her (Festus 245a).

LXII. This epithalamium, unlike LXI, was not written for a particular occasion: the atmosphere of the wedding-feast is Greek, but the imminent arrival of the bride reflects the Roman ceremony. A refrain indicates the division of the verses between the boys and the girls (who have banqueted at separate tables): the first nineteen lines set the scene and we are to understand them as snatches of talk from the young people preliminary to a choral competition, which begins at line 20. The contest naturally ends with the victory of the boys, who champion marriage. The textual tradition is marred by the loss of several lines, the substance of which, however, it is possible to restore from the strict symmetry of the composition.

1. *Olympus*, the great mountain in north-eastern Thessaly, home of the gods, but here as often simply denoting the sky.

7. *Oeta*, a mountain on the northern border of Aetolia conventionally associated with the rising of the evening star (the planet Venus).

LXIII. Worship of the Great Mother, Cybele, came to Rome from Asia Minor at the time of the Second Punic War: a temple was built on the Palatine in her honour, and by Catullus' day the orgiastic dancing of her priests had become a familiar spectacle in the streets of the city. Greek influence on Catullus' poem is revealed by setting, vocabulary, and metre; and he may also have owed something to native poets like Caecilius (xxxv), who took Cybele's cult for a theme. But the emotional involvement with which he handles the material is unmistakably his own.

The poem tells how Attis, a Greek youth, leaves home under an irresistible impulse, crosses the Aegean to Phrygian Ida and having castrated himself enters the service of the goddess, who never thereafter allows him to return. The irreversibility of his condition is arrestingly reflected by the employment of the feminine gender in referring to him (in the manuscript tradition these feminines have been systematically altered to the masculine except for the tell-tale instances where metre forbids this). Attis' extraordinary psychological situation is vividly dramatized in his two speeches; and at the end the poet starts up as if from a nightmare and cries out in fear.

2. *the Phrygian woodland,* of Mount Ida in the Troad (cf. 30).

12. *Gallae:* the male devotees of Cybele were known as *Galli,* and the feminine form (which does, however, occur in a Greek fragment) was probably contrived by Catullus to emphasize their emasculation.

13. *Dindymus,* a mountain in Phrygia (not far from the modern Ankara) dedicated to the cult of Cybele; and there is another mountain of the same name (or rather Dindymon) on the peninsula north of Cyzicus, where the Argonauts sacrificed to the goddess.

23. *Maenades:* the poet applies to the *Galli* a term which strictly refers to the female followers of Bacchus; but the two Asiatic cults were identified before Catullus.

hederigerae: this word, like other compounds in this poem and elsewhere in his work, is most probably a coinage by Catullus himself, the many short syllables suiting the metre (cf. 34 *properipedem,* 72 *nemorivagus*).

43. *Pasithea,* one of the Graces, promised in Homer, *Iliad* 14. 267ff as wife to Sleep.

77. *on the left,* as being the sinister side.

LXIV. The marriage of Peleus and Thetis, whose union Catullus was the first to ascribe to romantic love and depicts as both happy and sanctioned by heaven, frames the contrasting story of Theseus and Ariadne, centred wherein is the moving soliloquy of the deserted princess. The wedding itself concludes with a song of the three Fates foretelling the glorious career of Achilles; a repeated refrain divides their utterance into twelve parts (but see on 361), from which we are to understand that each of them sings a part in turn (like the three Norns in the prelude to Wagner's *Götterdämmerung*). There follows an epilogue lamenting mankind's present degeneracy from the virtuousness of the heroic age. The structure of the poem is symmetrical about Ariadne's soliloquy (ABCDEFEDCBA), but Catullus has—wisely—not shackled himself to a numerical congruence, as he did in LXVIII B.

This 'little epic' was probably intended to be the poet's masterpiece, rivalling Cinna's *Smyrna* (xcv). But for all its many felicities of detail and the care taken in its metrical technique, and in spite of its historical importance, for it greatly influenced Virgil and Ovid, the work does not attain the poetical excellence of Catullus' lyrics or elegiacs: his spontaneous and unaffected genius was ill-suited to the learned artificialities of the epyllion. Catullus cannot have thought of publishing it except as a separate *libellus*, and if he was indeed ready to send it out to the world in its present form, we cannot be sure of its title (those we know, from Callimachus' *Hecale* to the *Ciris*, are nearly all single names of females, and this would suggest *Ariadne*).

In his note on Lucretius 3.57 Munro has shown conclusively that in composing the Theseus and Ariadne episode Catullus has on some eleven occasions echoed distinctive phrases found in the *De Rerum Natura*; coincidence being out of the question, we are obliged to recognize Catullus as the borrower. Now Lucretius died towards the end of 55 and his work was published posthumously under the supervision of Cicero; the latter's brother Quintus read a copy early in 54. It seems as if Catullus read the work at the same time, for he was dead by the end of the year, and in between we must postulate the last stages in the composition of poem LXIV.

1. The ship Argo, which carried the Greek youths to Colchis (Aeetes was its king, Phasis its chief river) in quest of the Golden Fleece, was built under the guidance of Pallas Athena (8) from pines which grew on Mount Pelion in Thessaly.

11. *Amphitrite*, a Nereid (cf. on 30), wife of Neptune, and used by metonymy for the sea.

21. *Father*, Jupiter (26): he had fallen in love with Thetis, but yielded her to Peleus on learning (from Prometheus) that she was fated to bear a son greater than his father.

30. Thetis was the daughter of Nereus and his sister-wife Doris, who were children of Tethys and her brother-husband Oceanus.

35. *Cieros* (an emendation: the mss imply *Scyros*, an island in the Aegean, which cannot be right), *Crannon*, *Larissa*, *Pharsalus*: towns in Thessaly.

Tempe, the valley of the river Peneus in the north of Thessaly (far from Phthiotis, which is in the south: but Phthiotic is used by poetic licence as a synonym for Thessalian).

52. After killing the Minotaur Theseus sailed off with Ariadne to Dia: this for Catullus, as for Callimachus (frag. 601), is the older name for Naxos, the large island in the Cyclades roughly equidistant from Crete and Athens; but the name really belongs to an island a few miles off the Cnossian coast and still so called today.

72. *Lady of Eryx*, Venus, who had a famous temple on Mount Eryx in the western corner of Sicily.

74. *Piraeus*, the port of Athens.

75. *Gortynia*, Cretan, from Gortyn, the second city of the island.

77. Androgeon, son of Minos: on a visit to Athens he was murdered by rivals he had defeated at the Panathenaic Games (by Aegeus, say others); Minos promptly besieged Athens, which was forced to accept his terms when the land was visited by a cruel pestilence.

79. *Cecropia*, Athens, after Cecrops, its founder.

89. *Eurotas*, the river which flows south through Sparta to the Laconic Gulf.

96. *Golgi, Idalium*, cult-centres of Venus in Cyprus (cf. XXXVI 12, 14).

105. *Taurus*, the mountain range of Cilicia.

118. *consanguineae*, presumably Phaedra, who later became the wife of Theseus.

141. The line can be read as a combination of glyconic and pherecratean, the metre used for wedding songs, to which this is a pathetic allusion.

150. *brother*, the Minotaur: 'but that Ariadne should speak of him as her brother is an offence to us and ought to have been to Catullus' (Macnaghten).

156. The personification of three dangerous hazards for sailors: the Syrtes were shoals on the north African coast, and Scylla a rock and Charybdis a whirlpool on either side of the Straits of Messina.

172. *Cnosia*, Cretan, from Cnos(s)us, Minos' capital (a little to the south of Heracleon, modern Iraklion).

178. *Idaeus*, of her native Crete, the chief mountain being called Ida.

211. *Erechtheus* (Latin spells such Greek words with only the second aspirate, thus: *Erecteus*) was the great-grandfather of Aegeus, and hence Erechthean=Athenian.

217. Theseus was brought up at Troezen by his mother Aethra; only on reaching maturity did he journey to Athens and make himself known to his father.

228. *Itonus*, or Iton, a town in Phthiotic Thessaly, possessing a celebrated sanctuary of Athena.

249f. Reverting to the scene portrayed on the tapestry.

251. *Iacchus*, like Bacchus another name of Dionysus; born in Nysa (variously located, mostly in India), he was regularly attended by males, the satyrs young and wanton, the sileni old and drunk. His female followers, called Bacchants or Maenads or Thy(i)ads (the last two words mean 'frenzied women'), stimulated themselves with wine and the touch of the thyrsus, a vine-rod covered with ivy.

255ff. This description may be illustrated from various passages in Euripides' *Bacchae*. The caskets held sacred serpents and other paraphernalia of Dionysiac liturgy.

264. *barbara*, non-Greek: specifically, Phrygian.

279. *Chiron*, the wise centaur who lived on Mount Pelion and was destined to become Achilles' tutor.

282. *Favonius*, the West Wind or zephyr.

285. *Peneus*, the chief river in Thessaly, but here the river-god is meant.

287. *Haemonides*, a feminine toponymic from Haemonia, a poetical name for Thessaly.

291. *Phaethon*, unable to control the chariot of his father, the Sun, was blasted with a thunderbolt by Jupiter lest he set the earth on fire; his sisters, who had yoked the horses for him, were changed into poplars as a punishment.

294. *Prometheus*, the Titan who brought fire (and the arts) to mortals, for which he was chained to a rock on Mount Caucasus, the victim of an eagle who fed daily on his liver. He was released from this punishment when he revealed to Jupiter the danger inherent in marriage to Thetis (cf. on 21).

299. *Phoebus* (Apollo) and his sister (Diana = Artemis) absent themselves from the wedding as being partisans of Troy, he moreover being Achilles' destined killer.

300. *Idrus*, commonly assumed to be the founder of Idrias in Caria, a cult-centre of Hecate (= Diana), but the reading is probably corrupt.

306. *Parcae*: they are named in Hesiod, *Theogony* 905: Clotho, the spinner; Lachesis, the allotter of fate: and Atropos, the unavoidable, who cuts the thread. But various accounts are given of their functions, and Catullus represents them as working together.

324. *Emathia*, strictly Macedonia, but poetically used as a synonym of Thessaly; the son of Ops (the Italian counterpart of the Greek Rhea) is Jupiter, the phrase translating the Homeric 'dear to Zeus'.

344. *Teucrian*, Trojan, from Teucer, the first king of Troy.

346. *Pelops* broke his promise to give half his kingdom to Myrtilus, who helped him win the chariot-race by which he gained the hand of Hippodamia. Here Catullus probably has Homer in mind, according to whom (*Iliad* 2.105ff) Pelops left his sceptre to

Atreus, who left it to Thyestes, who left it to Agamemnon, thus third in line from Pelops.

357. *Scamander*, the chief river of Troyland, at which Achilles utterly routed the Trojans (Homer, *Iliad* 21).

361. Mueller conjectured that a stanza beginning *testis erit* and prophesying the slaying of Hector has been lost after this verse.

364. *weary*, with ten years' fighting.

367. *undo the coronal*, translating Homer's 'undo the sacred coronal of Troy' (*Iliad* 16.100), referring to the walls of the city, built by Neptune for Laomedon, father of Priam.

368. *Polyxena*, daughter of Priam and Hecuba, sacrificed over Achilles' tomb to appease his ghost, the climax of Euripides' *Hecuba* (in which, however, she is not beheaded, but has her throat cut).

376f. Among the ancients an old wives' tale held that the consummation of a marriage was confirmed by the bride's expanded neck-size.

390. *Parnassus*, the mountain overlooking Delphi and (among other things) a haunt of Bacchus (=Dionysus, Liber) and his female followers.

395. *Triton's mistress*, Athena, born on the river Triton (variously located), this translating Homer's enigmatic epithet Tritogenia.

Amarynthian maid, Diana (Artemis), from her cult-centre at Amarynthus in Euboea.

LXV–LXVIII. Though composed in the same metre as the epigrams which follow, the poems in this section are in style and tone much different from them, being by turns colloquial and erudite, artificial and heart-baring, but altogether lacking the tightness and sharpness of wit characteristic of epigram. We can now see clearly that Catullus was groping his way towards an elegiac genre of personal love-poetry, which was only established with Gallus and his fellow Augustans.

LXV. A one-sentence (cf. II) letter to Quintus Hortensius Hortalus (114–50), the famous orator and Cicero's chief rival, written by the poet shortly after his brother's death and accompanying a translation (LXVI) from Callimachus, the most distinguished descendant of Battus (VII 6). Rhoeteum was a promontory in the Troad. The Daulian bird is Procne, wife of Tereus, king of Daulis: maddened by his violence to her sister Philomela, she slew her son Itylus (more usually Itys) and was condemned, as a nightingale, to sing a perpetual lament for him.

LXVI. Shortly after her marriage (247) Queen Berenice of Egypt vowed a lock of her hair to the gods if her husband, Ptolemy III Euergetes, returned safe from war. When he did, she duly fulfilled her promise, but the next morning—horror!—the lock had vanished. A scandal was averted when Conon, the court astronomer and evidently a diplomat of parts, discovered it as a new constellation in the sky. The whole story, as told by the lock of hair itself, was promptly versified by Callimachus (some thirty lines from the relevant portion of the *Aetia* are preserved in two papyri—for an English translation see page 195); this then is the poem here translated by Catullus.

5f. During interlunation the Moon (Trivia, cf. XXXIV 15f) is fancied to be secretly meeting Endymion in the cave on Mount Latmos in Caria where he lies asleep.

22. Actually Ptolemy was Berenice's cousin.

27. Berenice's mother Apame opposed her betrothal to Ptolemy and promised her to Demetrius, brother of the king of Macedonia. When he became her mother's lover, however, Berenice had him assassinated and married the man of her choice.

44. Boreas, the North Wind, son of Aurora (Eos: the Dawn), daughter of Hyperion and Thia.

46. *Athos*, not strictly the highest peak in the north (Olympus and others are higher); and Xerxes' canal (483 B.C.) was cut through the isthmus twenty-five miles north-west of the mountain.

48. *Chalybes*, the legendary discoverers and workers of iron, whose name in historical times was borne by a tribe on the southern shore of the Black Sea.

52ff. The Lock was carried to heaven by Zephyrus, the West Wind, like Memnon a son of Aurora, and here seemingly represented as an ostrich. He acts as the messenger of the deified Arsinoe (second wife of Ptolemy II), worshipped after her death as Venus (Aphrodite), and to whose temple on the promontory of Zephyrium (a Locrian foundation between Alexandria and Canopus) the Lock was first transferred (56) from the Pantheon in which it was initially deposited.

60f. The constellation Corona Borealis is usually held to be the golden crown given by Bacchus to Ariadne at their wedding.

65f. The Lock of Berenice is the group of stars found in the area bounded by the constellations Virgo, Leo, Ursa Major (the bear into which Callisto, Lycaon's daughter, was transformed and given apotheosis), and Bootes (who takes hours to set because of his vertical position).

70. *Tethys*, wife of Ocean, the sea surrounding the world, and hence the horizon.

71. *Rhamnusian maid*, Nemesis, so called after her famous temple at Rhamnus in Attica; she is invoked as the deity whose function it is to punish human presumption.

94. The constellation Orion is separated by a vast stretch of sky from Aquarius (who is Ganymede, an attractive youth).

LXVII. Caecilius (cf. xxxv) has just acquired a house at Verona, the scene of some scandalous conduct which the poet here unfolds. It had been occupied by the younger Balbus, who married a girl from Brixia (conceivably the principals of xvii); her previous marriage was terminated before being consummated, but she was not a virgin when she entered the house. Far from it: her Brixian father-in-law had seduced her, and she had other lovers, among them one unnamed (though he is described precisely enough), who seems to be the real target of the piece: he had been taken to court for attempting to secure possession of his father-in-law's estate by feigning the birth of a son to his wife. Though Catullus does not assert an interest, his defamation is most naturally explained as coming from the lips of a rejected suitor; and in fact the poem forms an unusual variation of the paraclausithyron, the song of the excluded lover outside his beloved's door, which may, as here, receive abuse and be given a speaking role.

1. The house-door is addressed as the guardian of a wife's chastity and a daughter's virginity.

31ff. *Brixia*, modern Brescia, to the west of which runs the river Mella, is just under forty miles west of Verona. It was the capital of the Cenomani, a Gallic tribe who may have founded Verona, and was situated beneath a peak named after Cycnus, a Ligurian prince whose grief for Phaethon (LXIV 291) caused him to be changed into a swan. The unexpected geographical and historical information given suggests that Catullus was poking fun, as a Veronese might well, at the pretensions of the Brixians.

46. *in case he raises*, sc. in anger.

LXVIII A. On the news of his brother's death (perhaps early in 59) Catullus hurried to his home in Verona. Sometime thereafter Manlius, presumably he whose wedding is celebrated in LXI, wrote him a letter urging him to return to Rome at once in view of Clodia's behaviour: diplomatically endeavouring to blunt the blow, he tells Catullus of unhappiness he himself is suffering from setbacks in his love-life and begs him for the poem he had earlier been promised. The poet's reply reveals him as too shattered by his brother's death to turn his mind to serious composition. However, he later relented and fulfilled the request in LXVIII B (a separate poem).

10. What Manlius requested was a poetic composition of Catullus' combining both the theme of love and the learning appropriate to neoteric verse.

15. About the age of sixteen a Roman boy donned the plain white toga of manhood, discarding the child's robe, which was edged with purple.

27f. Manlius (who wrote from Rome) is insisting that in Verona Catullus, like other young aristocrats, could not engage in amorous pursuits with the same freedom possible in the capital.

LXVIII B. This, the most studied of Catullus' elegiac poems, immortalizes the service of the friend who provided an establishment where the poet could meet his mistress. Catullus, however, camouflages his name, to avoid, it may be, the danger of implicating this friend in his adultery; but, not to mention the repetition of some verses from LXVIII A, the disguise is easily penetrated, for on its first occurrence the elision of *me* before *Allius* approximates to the colloquial pronunciation of Manlius. The composition is arranged with an elaborate symmetry extending even to the number of verses in the constituent parts.

51. *Amathusia*, of Amathus (cf. XXXVI 14), i.e. Venus.

53. *Trinacria rupes*, literally, the crag of the three-cornered island: Etna.

54. *lympha*, the hot springs which gave Thermopylae ('gate of hot springs') its name; Oeta (LXII 7) is the name of the mountain on which Thermopylae is situated, and Malis that of the district.

65. *Castor and Pollux*, cf. on IV 27.

74ff. *Protesilaus* was the first of the Greeks to die at Troy (=*Ilium*, 86), having married Laodamia shortly before the sacrifice of Iphigenia (=*hostia*, 76: so Richard Thomas) enabled the expedition to sail from Aulis.

77. *Rhamnusian maid*, Nemesis, cf. on LXVI 71.

109ff. Underground channels near the town of Pheneus at the foot of Mount Cyllene in Arcadia which drained off flood-waters from the river Olbios are said by Greek legend to have been dug by Hercules, the reputed son of Amphitryon, king of Thebes.

113ff. Hercules' fifth labour was the slaying of the man-eating birds which infested Lake Stymphalus (about ten miles west of Pheneus). His unworthy master was Eurystheus of Argos. On the completion of his labours he was raised to heaven and given Hebe for wife, the goddess of youth.

125ff. The conjugal felicity of doves is proverbial.

133. Cupid's presence suggests that Clodia was Venus personified.

148. The turn of speech probably derives from the practice of denoting happy days on the calendar with a chalk-mark (cf. CVII 7).

LXVIII C. The symmetrical structure of LXVIII B demonstrates that what follows was considered by the poet a separate composition; and we have no guarantee that he envisaged publication for it. 'Your true-love' is presumably Junia Aurunculeia (LXI); 'he of Africa' (if the reading is correct) is a pseudonym for Caelius Rufus, who had in 60 returned from Africa (where he had served on the governor's staff as Catullus was to do in Bithynia).

LXIX–CXVI. Whereas we may feel confident that the arrangement of the hendecasyllabic poems is in large measure Catullus' own, the same assurance is not possible in the case of the epigrams. Some design is certainly discernible, but after about LXXXVII what clues there are (e.g. the uncharacteristic clustering of LXXXVIII–XCI, the inconsequent placement of CI, the incomplete nature of CII) point rather to the editor.

Of the themes to be found in this section Catullus' love affair with Lesbia greatly predominates: an intelligible series is formed by LXX, LXXII, LXXIII, LXXV, and LXXVI; then Lesbia plays either the leading or a major role in LXXVIIIB, LXXIX, LXXXII, LXXXIII, LXXXV, LXXXVI, LXXXVII, XCI, XCII, and CIV; and finally, two epigrams written in reconciliation, CVII and CIX. Next there is a cycle of invective against Gellius: LXXIV, LXXX, LXXXVIII, LXXXIX, XC, XCI, and CXVI. The remainder, apart from a few pairs (LXIX, LXXI; CX, CXI; CXIV, CXV), are casual, disconnected pieces.

LXIX. No doubt aimed at the same target as LXXI, probably Caelius Rufus, and if so, wildly hyperbolical, for he is known to have been a ladies' man.

LXX. Clodia's husband Metellus died in March, 59.

LXXI. Another attempt (see LXIX) to ridicule Rufus. Quintius (whose name is here conjectured) recurs in LXXXII and C.

LXXII. Since the date of LXX, to which the first couplet alludes, the affair has gone further downhill.

LXXIII. This poem of despair foreshadows the more elaborate LXXVI. In the last line the manuscript tradition gives *qui* ('than *he* who but now had in me *his* . . .'), and this has generally been referred to Caelius Rufus (LXXVII), who supplanted Catullus as Clodia's lover. But the unique degree of friendship expressed in the last line (the five elisions compel a breathless utterance such as is consonant with deep emotion) points rather to the *sancta amicitia* of CIX.

LXXIV. The first in the collection (though perhaps not in order of composition) of a cycle of abusive epigrams against Lucius Gellius Publicola, who moved in the same circle as Clodius and Caelius Rufus. His father Lucius Gellius (consul 72) had divorced his mother and married Palla, whom Catullus negligently refers to as Gellius' mother. At all events Gellius was later accused of seducing her (a senate hearing absolved him). Palla, divorced again, then married Marcus Valerius Messalla (consul 61), who already had a daughter Valeria old enough to fit (counting stepsisters as sisters) Catullus' allegations. As for Uncle Gellius, Cicero in a fierce attack on him (*Pro Sestio* 110ff) speaks insinuatingly of his wife as a *libertina*. Finally, Gellius' brother-in-law was the man who prosecuted Caelius in the case instigated by Clodia, which makes it probable that Clodia and Gellius were acquainted. In the civil war he tried to assassinate Brutus and Cassius but was foiled; surviving this hazard he became consul in 36 and met his end in 31, commanding a wing of Antony's fleet at Actium.

4. *Harpocrates* is an Egyptian sun-god, represented as a boy holding his left forefinger to his lips to enjoin silence (also CII).

LXXV. A further development of the theme of LXXII.

LXXVI. This, the second of Catullus' soliloquies (cf. VIII), expresses in elegiac form (comparable with LXV–LXVIII) the despair voiced epigrammatically in LXXXV. All thought of reconciliation has been abandoned, and the poet is close to a final repudiation, to which he commits himself in his second Sapphic (XI). That this lay in his thoughts is suggested by the poignant echoes in 19–21 of the first Sapphic (LI 5–10).

LXXVII.   The addressee can hardly be other than Caelius Rufus, of whose affair with Clodia we learn also from Cicero's speech in his defence. The echo in line 4 of LXVIIIC 158 suggests a date of composition not long after that poem; and in the last line Catullus must be principally thinking of his love for his sweetheart.

LXXVIII.   It is tempting to compare this with LXXIV and to conclude that the charming son is Gellius and Gallus his uncle.

LXXVIII B.   The general sense of the supplement is obvious enough, but the name of the villain is lost in the lacuna. However, the woman whom Catullus defends so hotly can only be Lesbia, and the eternal dishonour attendant upon this encounter suggests that the poet's accusation is incest—exactly as in the following poem.

LXXIX.   Lesbius is a transparent pseudonym for Publius Clodius Pulcher, Clodia's brother and a thoroughly odious character: Cicero, too, accuses the pair of having incestuous relations.

LXXX.   Victor is not a republican cognomen, and may here serve as a pseudonym. For Gellius, see LXXIV.

LXXXI.   Perhaps Aurelius (cf. xv) is here referred to? Pisaurum (Pesaro), a town of Umbria, lies on the coast twenty miles south-east of Ariminum (Rimini).

LXXXII.   An appeal to Quintius (C and perhaps also in LXXI) not to steal Lesbia from him.

LXXXIII.   Lesbia's husband is still alive (see note on LXX).

LXXXIV.   Quintus Arrius is mentioned by Cicero (*Brutus* 242) as an uneducated orator: he became an aide of Crassus, who went out to Syria in November, 55.
The Latin aspirate had become by the first century a very weak sound, the Italians having a natural tendency (today fully gratified) to get rid of it. But Greek influence and social pretension combined strongly to rehabilitate it, not only in those words where it belonged but even in others where it did not (e.g. *pulcher*). Catullus (like Cicero) was one who resisted the fashion and derived some amusement from excesses it occasioned.

LXXXV.   The culmination of LXX, LXXII, LXXIII, and LXXV.

LXXXVI.   Quintia is perhaps the sister of Quintius (LXXXII, C) and evidently worthier of comparison with Lesbia than the girl from Anneianum (XLIII).

LXXXVII.   The lack of point, together with the abrupt shift of Lesbia from third to second person, proclaims this to be a fragment not ready for publication. Even so, it stands as a clear expression of Catullus' fallacious belief that love is a matter of contract.

LXXXVIII.   Remarkably in our collection this and the next three poems all deal with the same person: see also LXXIV, LXXX, and CXVI. Tethys (5) is the wife of Oceanus (6) and, like him, here represents the sea.

LXXXIX.   The same theme continued.

XC.   Strabo (15.735) mentions the practice of incestuous marriages among Persian soothsayers.

XCI.   The additional charge against Gellius, that he has enjoyed Lesbia's favours, may furnish the real cause of Catullus' invectives against him.

XCII.   Seemingly of the same period as LXXXIII.

XCIII.   Apparently written after an attempt by Caesar to conciliate the poet.

XCIV.   Mamurra's nickname is established from XXIX. Its first occurrence here stands as a proper name, while the second bears its ordinary connotation. The saying is otherwise unknown.

XCV.   Cinna's *Smyrna* (a little epic on the same scale as LXIV) is favourably compared with the *Annals* of Volusius (XXXVI), whose turgidity rivals that of Antimachus of Colophon, a fifth-century poet who wrote a *Thebaid*. For Cinna, see further X and CXIII. Hatria, the native town of Volusius, is situated in the Po delta, one mouth of which is the Padua.
  Smyrna (or Myrrha) conceived an uncontrollable passion for her father Cinyras, king of Cyprus (Satrachus is a river in that island): the story is told in the sixth book of Ovid's *Metamorphoses*.
  The heroine's name is spelt *Zmyrna* in the manuscripts and editions, a

spelling which undoubtedly goes back to the days of Catullus and beyond; it reflects the contemporary pronunciation of the name of the great city. But in classical Greek literature the name was invariably spelt with *s*; and it is this spelling, insisted on by the grammarian Priscian (*GL* 2.23 and 41), which was probably employed by Cinna. Similarly in LXVIII the contemporary spelling *Laudamia* has ousted Catullus' (the classical Greek) form, which, however, is required by the metre.

XCVI. Scholars dispute whether Quintilia was wife or mistress, but her identity as Calvus' literary sweetheart is established by Propertius (2.34.89f), who places her in the company of Catullus' Lesbia and Gallus' Lycoris.

XCVII. Aemilius is not known, but the coarseness of the abuse suggests that this, like the following (the two were designedly placed together in the collection: compare line 9 of this with line 4 of that), is a political lampoon. The hangman is specified as the crudest and cruellest of men.

XCVIII. Lucius Vettius was a notorious informer (in 62 he had accused Caesar of involvement in the Catilinarian conspiracy) who died in prison in 59 after an unsuccessful attempt to implicate a number of leading senators in a plot to murder Pompey. But the name may here be used as a pseudonym.

XCIX. The longest, and perhaps the first, of the Juventius poems. Note the first and last words: this framing, and the narrative style of the poem generally, mark it as having, like LXXVI, more in common with Catullus' elegiac than with his epigrammatic compositions.

C. Actually Caelius was not born in Verona, but in the context of this poem he is considered as a resident. The point of the epigram lies in its intense irony: Caelius and Quintius have already been associated as lovers of Lesbia (LXXI, LXXXII); and we have also learnt (from LXXVII) how the former's friendship stood up to the crucial test.

Perhaps written in 55, when Crassus passed a law against political *sodalicia* or brotherhoods. The theme of brotherly love led the editor to place, to a modern taste insensitively, this and the following poem together.

    5. *You of course, Caelius:* sc. I don't think!

CI. On his journey to Bithynia Catullus took the opportunity to visit his brother's grave in the Troad, where, so he implies, he composed this last tribute to him. The actual offerings 'moistened with a brother's many tears' were, to judge from Tibullus 2.6.32, a garland of flowers. Repeated use of the letter *m* helps to create a mood of mourning.

Many editors, following the perverse lead of the author of the *Ciris* (42ff), construe the *quandoquidem* clause with lines 7–10 (but the connection between lines 4 and 5 is 'that I may address your dead ashes, not being able to address your living self').

CII. These lines are no more than a private communication in verse and were hardly written with a view to publication. Only the addressee can have known the circumstances or treasured the poem enough to preserve it (for it proclaims the poet's intimacy with him); and it is natural to identify him with Cornelius Nepos (1), who thus will in all probability have been Catullus' editor. For Harpocrates, see on LXXIV.

CIII. Silo is otherwise unknown. The amount mentioned is that asked for by the girl from Anneianum (XLI), and some have thought Silo her agent.

CIV. The poet's denial hardly squares with XCII. In the manuscripts the last line reads *sed tu cum Tappone omnia monstra facis* 'but there is no enormity that you and Tappo shrink from'. Yet in this the addressee is unidentified; and the gibe was probably directed against the proper name. It is found in inscriptions but may here be a pseudonym ('you clown'), for it seems to have been borne by a stock character in Italian farce.

CV. Mamurra's literary pretensions are also alluded to in LVII. Pipla is the name of a spring on the northern slopes of Mount Olympus.

CVI. Perhaps Juventius attended by Aurelius (XXI 5f): 'Thus does Juventius, if indeed this be he, disappear from our view' (McDaniel).

CVII. The artifice of verbal repetition has contributed much to the ecstatic tone of this poem, whether marking a reunion in early days (with 6 compare LXVIII B 148) or a reconciliation after estrangement (like that indicated in XXXVI).

CVIII. The butt of this invective, drawn on by Ovid (*Ibis* 165ff), may have been one of two brothers from Spoletum mentioned by Cicero (*Pro Cluentio* 100ff).

CIX.   This epigram follows closely on CVII, that marking the first rapture of reunion, this the sobering reflection that it may not last.

CX.   Against the lady once wooed by Quintius (c).

CXI.   The poet manages to cap the charge made in CX.

CXII.   A pun on the meanings of *multus*: 'meddlesome' (i.e. a busybody) and 'many a'. Naso is not otherwise known.

CXIII.   Mucia, Pompey's third wife (Mucilla is a familiar diminutive used contemptuously), was divorced by him in 62 on his return from the East on the grounds of her adultery with Caesar: Pompey's first consulship was held in 70, his second in 55. It is not implied that the two original lovers are identical with the two mentioned in the third verse. As with the apostrophe to Cato in LVI, there is no special point in addressing Cinna (x).

CXIV.   Mamurra's estate at Firmum, a town in Picenum south of Ancona, is vast but a drain on his resources.

CXV.   A variation on the preceding. The inordinate exaggeration that the estate stretches as far as the Northern Ocean is designed to pave the way for the (rather feeble) conclusion.

 5.   The strange corruption in the manuscripts comes from a misguided attempt to heal the haplography *silvas⟨vas⟩tasque*.

CXVI.   Perhaps the first shot fired at Gellius (see LXXIV), placed here, last in the collection, not by any design of Catullus', but simply because it was the last epigram to come to the editor's desk. The Battiad is Callimachus, as at LXV 16. In the last line the elision of *s* plays on Romulus' threat to murder Remus (in Ennius): *nam mi calido dabi' sanguine poenas* 'you will pay me the penalty with your life-blood' (Timpanaro).

Select Bibliography

Standard editions

C. Valerius Catullus, edited by Wilhelm Kroll (German: introduction, text, apparatus, commentary, addenda to 1922 edition), Teubner, Stuttgart 1968⁵. Contains full bibliography for 1929–67 by J. Kroymann.

Catullus, edited by Elmer Truesdell Merrill (introduction, text, commentary, critical appendix), Boston 1893 (now Harvard repr. 1951).

C. Valerii Catulli Carmina, edited by R. A. B. Mynors (text and apparatus: *Oxford Classical Texts*), Oxford 1958.

Catullus/The Poems, edited by Kenneth Quinn (introduction, text, commentary), Macmillan 1970.

Other editions and commentaries

Baehrens, Aemilius: *Catulli Veronensis Liber* (Latin: prolegomena, commentary), Leipzig 1885. A landmark in the textual criticism of the poet.

Ellis, Robinson: *A Commentary on Catullus* (prolegomena, commentary), Oxford 1889².

Fordyce, C. J.: *Catullus/A Commentary* (text and apparatus from Mynors' *OCT*: introduction, commentary; but omits text and commentary for 32 poems), Oxford 1961, 1973².

McDaniel 2d, W. B.: *The Poems of Catullus* (introduction, text, notes: arranged in conjectural chronological order), New York 1931.

Pighi, Giovanni Battista: *Catullo Veronese*, 3 volumes (I Prolegomena; II Testo Latino; III Testo Italiano), Verona 1961. Nonpareil. Magnificently produced and lavishly illustrated, vol. I with black and white photographs, vols II and III with colour reproductions of ancient paintings.

Thomson, D. F. S.: *Catullus/A Critical Edition* (introduction on and list of 146 manuscripts, text, apparatus), Chapel Hill 1978.

Facsimile

Catullus: Carmina, Codex Oxoniensis Bibliothecae Bodleianae Canonicianus Class. Lat. 30, with a preface by R. A. B. Mynors (*Codices Graeci et Latini Phototypice Depicti* XXI), Leiden 1966.

English verse translations

Lindsay, Jack: *Catullus/The Complete Poems* ... with introduction and commentary (arranged in conjectured chronological order), Silvan Press, London 1948.

Macnaghten, Hugh: *The Poems of Catullus*, Cambridge 1925. Gives Latin as well as English, but omits 40 poems and some other verses.

Studies

Havelock, E. A.: *The Lyric Genius of Catullus*, Oxford 1939 (repr. New York 1967).

Munro, H. A. J.: *Criticisms and Elucidations of Catullus*, Cambridge 1878, 1905².

Neudling, Chester Louis: *A Prosopography to Catullus*, Oxford 1955 (*Iowa Studies in Classical Philology*, Number 12).

Quinn, Kenneth: *The Catullan Revolution*, Melbourne 1959.

Quinn, Kenneth: *Catullus: An Interpretation*, London 1972.

Ross Jr, David O.: *Style and Tradition in Catullus*, Cambridge, Massachusetts 1969. Finds the epigrams to be lacking in neoteric mannerisms.

Wetmore, Munro Nichols: *Index Verborum Catullianus*, New Haven 1912 (repr. 1961).

Wheeler, Arthur Leslie: *Catullus and the Traditions of Ancient Poetry*, Berkeley and Los Angeles 1934 (*Sather Classical Lectures* IX). An introduction to Catullus.

Wilamowitz-Moellendorff, Ulrich von: *Hellenistische Dichtung*, 2 vols, Berlin 1924 (repr. 1962). Volume II, chapter 8 (pp. 227–310): *Catulls hellenistische Gedichte*.

Wiseman, T. P.: *Catullan Questions*, Leicester 1969. A challenge to several orthodox beliefs.

Nachleben and bibliography

Duckett, Eleanor Shipley: *Catullus in English Poetry*, Northampton, Massachusetts 1925 (*Smith College Classical Studies*, Number 6).

Harrington, Karl Pomeroy: *Catullus and his Influence*, Boston 1923.

McPeek, James A. S.: *Catullus in Strange and Distant Britain*, Cambridge, Massachusetts 1939 (*Harvard Studies in Comparative Literature*, Volume XV).

Harrauer, Hermann: *A Bibliography to Catullus*, Hildesheim 1977. Lists under seventeen sections some three thousand titles (dating from 1472 to 1977), followed by three indices: (a) *locorum*, (b) *rerum et verborum*, (c) *virorum doctorum*.